THE TRAP DOOR

CINDY LAFAVRE YORKS

This book is dedicated to anyone and everyone who found themselves down and out in the abyss and in desperate need of a savior.

TABLE OF CONTENTS

INTRODUCTION

Many of you reading this second book in The Door series have already ventured with me through *The Side Door*. It's a detour we never see coming that is designed to prompt growth and refinement. It may last for a short time or a lifetime.

But when we fall through a trap door, we are even more off guard. We may be plodding down a carefully chosen course that appears innocuous or perhaps even promising. Wind in our sails, we press forward in life, looking ahead—but perhaps not always entirely around. Maybe we're even a little complacent about our journey. We take a shortcut here, cut a corner there. We neglect to consult our Navigator or put our armor on. We take a few missteps. And then, suddenly, we've slipped into the abyss. It's in that moment that we come face to face with our Redeemer. He stands with us in the crossroads. He invites us to appeal to Him for an informed course correction. He recalculates our route, offering alternatives to enable us to finish the race marked out for us (Hebrews 12:1).

Join me as I lay out an inventory of trap doors the Enemy cleverly sets before us all. Pick up your proverbial stick and bandana with me as I share my packing tips for the journey. Grab your compass as I lay out a divinely inspired itinerary for the mind, soul, and body. I'll guide you on how to cope with unexpected pitfalls and show you how to avoid impulses to "go rogue." By seeking His will and following His leading, you will learn how to soar over seemingly insurmountable obstacles with newfound courage and confidence.

¡*Vaya con Dios*!
Cindy

WEEK 1: THE TRAP DOOR

THE TRAP DOOR: PRIDE

*M*y special needs son lives in his very own house on Altura Street. For you non–Spanish speakers, *altura* refers to "an elevated height." His dwelling and his caregiving were prayed over long before he ever set foot inside, a true testimony to God's Jeremiah 29:11 plan for his life. I love to tell the story of how we found this house, closed on it, and moved Max in within a miraculous ten-day period. It truly is one of the most amazing God stories of my life, and I feel a tremendous amount of joy whenever I am privileged to tell it.

I wish I could also tell you that giving glory to God is my natural storytelling default. But the truth is that pride, like the naughty teeth of a mischievous puppy, sometimes gets a foothold in my life. It can eradicate the edification that belongs to Him. Does this embarrassing default to edifying "self" ever happen to you?

Recently, I reached out to one Max's caregivers. I had not seen her in a while and thought it might be nice to take her and my son to lunch on her next shift. She had shared some of her personal struggles earlier in the year and asked me to pray for her. As I was driving over for the lunch date, I was in self-congratulatory mode, patting myself on the back, puffed up about what a noble deed I was undertaking.

When I arrived, she was in glorious spirits and authentic "gratitude mode." Her life was going well, and she was giving

God the glory. Then, she asked me how I was doing. In my desire to camp in that same authenticity, I shared honestly about my struggles as the mom of an adult special needs child whose behavior can be as volatile and frightening as a hurricane map in Indian summer. Without missing a beat, she began to remind me in Bible verse after Bible verse about God's purposes for Max—in the world, in my life, and in the life to come—in uplifting and powerful ways. There were tears of sadness and eventually joy. We enjoyed a nice lunch with Max, who was thankfully well-behaved that day.

After I hugged her, got in my car, and drove away, I realized the lunch was not at all the experience I expected. The supposedly needy caregiver turned out to be the one offering wisdom, knowledge, and—well, the care I needed. So much for my pride-filled image of the rescuing crusader.

The first human sin was committed out of prideful disobedience. Eve wanted knowledge of good and evil like God. Many if not most other sins also stem from pride—feeling superior to others; demanding superior treatment, validation, or privileges; blaming others or refusing accountability; and living a self-focused life. We must maintain a humble posture of continually questioning our own motivations. Then we can recalibrate our journey with small corrections instead of making continual U-turns.

⊢—⊸⊖

Keys to Kingdom Living: Suppress prideful tendencies and cultivate a posture of authentic humility.
Doorpost: "For the sin of their mouths, the words of their lips, let them be trapped in their pride." Psalm 59:12

THE TRAP DOOR: COMPARISON

*A*t the height of the conspicuous consumption of the '80s, luxury goods were at the zenith of their popularity. I remember someone actually sent our fashion department in LA a box of Louis Vuitton–printed garbage bags! This was an obvious trademark infringement!—but I digress.

When covering the prestigious New York designer fashion shows, it was common for a promotional freebie to be left on the chairs of the fashion editors. These would range from innocuous notepads and decals to more elaborate items such as scarves or totes. Because we editors traveled around in packs, seeing who might have received a T-shirt versus, say, a glazed leather bucket bag was not hard to do. One gal was particularly keen on seeing who received what, so for fun I devised a little prank. After the shows one night, I playfully inquired, "Didn't you just love the quilted Chanel coin purse?"

We snickered at her wide-eyed expression as she declared that no, indeed, she hadn't. I'd clued the others in prior to the stunt, but the next day we admitted we were pulling her leg. She was a little miffed at first, but we all laughed it off later.

As time went on and the economy tanked, chair candy dwindled in the publication row. VIP chair occupants shifted to a more *au courant* level of fashion show real estate, social media influencers, reminding us of yet another comparative truth: the playing field always levels out eventually.

Comparing cars, homes, colleges, kids, physiques, social media stats, or anything else is counterproductive to our social and spiritual development and well-being. It isn't God who compares and contrasts His children; comparison cards are the Devil's game. He uses culture, competition, advertising, dating websites, beauty contests, SAT scores, scholarships, "likes," and social status as his weapons, pitting us against each other. Meanwhile, our loving God tells us in His Word that we are wonderfully made, in Psalm 139:14. Instead of comparing a head of silky hair against another waning away from chemotherapy, Jesus instead tells us that God knows how many hairs are on each of our heads (Matthew 10:30). Instead of comparing the perfect hourglass body with the pear-shaped female, He instead collectively refers to us as "the apple of His eye," from Proverbs 7:2. Together, we are not to be contrasted—but instead, we unite to form what Peter refers to in 1 Peter 2:9 as "a royal priesthood, a holy nation."

Comparative thinking sets a trap for us to remain caught up in believing that we aren't enough: not pretty enough, not smart enough, not successful enough, or whatever "not enough" you find yourself obsessing over. It is true that we live in a broken world and won't achieve perfection this side of eternity. But God easily can and does supplement His "enough" for our "not quite," regardless of what our neighbor has more or less of than we do. And since we are made in His image, as we are reminded in Genesis 5:2, it's inappropriate to internalize a "less than" self-image. If anything, we can see some of our perceived deficiencies as a place for God to fill in the gap. As Paul acknowledged in 2 Corinthians 12:9, God's strength was made perfect in his own weakness. Indeed, God's grace is more than sufficient to render any comparison card as ineffective as a joker.

⊢•••෯

Keys to Kingdom Living: Forgo the compare card, instead internalizing the inimitable, unconditional love of our Lord Jesus.

Doorpost: "For we are God's masterpiece. He has created us anew in Christ Jesus, so we can do good things He planned for us long ago." Ephesians 2:10 (NLT)

THE TRAP DOOR: ABUNDANCE &
SELF-RELIANCE

rank Sinatra's "My Way" spells out the singer's cavalier approach to living life on his own terms. In his famous song, he makes this arrogant declaration: "For what is a man, what has he got? / If not himself then he has naught / To say the things he truly feels / And not the words of one who kneels . . ."[1]

Old Blue Eyes apparently wasn't too familiar with his Bible when he penned that pompous ditty, or he would have known that one day he will join every living creature in taking a knee before the Son of Man when He comes again in glory (Revelation 22:1-5). Sinatra was certainly not the only man or woman of renown to proudly eschew reliance on God or anyone else. Shirley MacLaine said, "I don't need anyone to rectify my existence. The most profound relationship we will ever have is the one with ourselves."[2] Sadder still is the partially true quote from American actor Kip Pardue who said, "I don't need anyone else, which is a great feeling, but also a depressing one."[3]

What could be more depressing than living out of relationship and communion with God? We are wired for relationship with Him. That relationship centers on our humility, deference, obedience, and the solid awareness that we are subjects and He is our King. Yet, historically, people have mocked God and been ensnared by their foolish pride. In 1911, a foolhardy spokesperson from the British shipping company the White Star

Line was asked by a reporter how safe the company's new ship would be. His answer? "Not even God Himself can sink this ship!" (We all know what happened to the *Titanic*.)

Of course, there are plenty of people walking the face of the earth who aren't as vocal as the aforementioned folks, yet still choose self-reliance over God-reliance. And even some Christians find themselves slipping into traps of self-reliance in their behavior and deeds from time to time. When we worry, we chose doubt over trust—it's an outward symbol of an inward power struggle. When we refuse to tithe during a financial crisis, we show that we value our own judgment and perceived logic over God's design regarding provision. When physicians try to manipulate the beginning of life itself or the exact timing of an individual's death, they teeter dangerously close to the Creator's sacred territory. And whenever we step out of obedience to God's laws, we set ourselves up as kings of our own kingdom of rebellion against the only King of Kings and Lord of Lords.

Though they may be subtler in nature, our little fiefdoms aren't any less offensive to God. Even if we declare our allegiance and profess our love for Him, we must constantly be on guard against any illusions we give ourselves that we don't need Him. We must never delude ourselves that our ways are higher than His. In 2 Timothy 3:1-2 we are reminded that "there will be terrible times in the last days. People will be lovers of themselves, lovers of money, boastful, proud, abusive, disobedient to their parents, ungrateful, unholy." We must commit to avoiding these traps as we persevere in our faithful journey on the path to glory. Though the road is filled with potential pitfalls, God promises that if we are faithful to Him, He will present us with a crown of life (Revelation 2:10).

꜔—•⬦

Keys to Kingdom Living: Don't allow a trap of self-sufficiency and success to distort your perception; strive to remain committed to a full reliance on God.

Doorpost: "Again I tell you, it is easier for a camel to go through the eye of a needle than for someone who is rich to enter the kingdom of God." Luke 18:24

THE TRAP DOOR: ENTITLEMENT

*T*he egregious scandals surrounding entrance into many of America's elite colleges are enough to make hard-working scholars—and perhaps their parents—bristle with righteous indignation. And to be fair, it's hard to argue with the fact that Instagram influencer Olivia Jade Giannuli's imaginary rowing prowess displaced other meritorious would-be contenders. And then there are her comments about education in general. In April 2017, she said in a tweet from her now-deleted Twitter account that "it's so hard to try in school when you don't care about anything you're learning."

Ethicists are having a field day dissecting today's rampant entitlement culture. Indeed, many books have been penned on the subject. Richard and Linda Eyre's *The Entitlement Trap* offers antidotes to entitlement that shatter the notion of deservedness. Their book offers a blueprint for implanting the value of responsibility, a sense of sufficiency, and personal accountability.

Of course, entitlement is hardly a new concept under the sun. In Numbers 11:1-9, the Israelites complained about the monotony of the manna that God provided every day, implying that they were entitled to the fish, cucumbers, melons, leeks, onions, and garlic given to them in Egypt. They even went so far as to say their "soul [was] dried away" (Numbers 11:6). How conveniently they'd forgotten their liberation from slavery as they focused on their culinary constraints. Then there was King

David, who considered himself to be "entitled" to Bathsheba, even though she was another man's wife. The apostle Thomas verbalized that he felt personally entitled to concrete proof that Jesus was indeed resurrected, choosing not to take the word of the other disciples.

Christianity actually involves the antithesis of entitlement. "He who is last will be first, and he who is first will be last," Jesus declares in Matthew 20:16. Sacrifice is at the root of every action or statement Jesus made the entire time He walked the face of the earth. We are called to do the same in this world. Jesus never promises a primrose lane, but instead reminds us in John 16:33 that "in this world, you will have trouble, but take heart! I have overcome the world." God doesn't play favorites. He welcomes all believers but will not welcome arrogant, hard of heart, entitled "posers." Misinformed people who think their self-motivated good deeds or the solid faith traditions of their parents or grandparents entitle them to a pass to eternity will be gravely mistaken when Jesus separates the sheep from the goats. Their entitlement attitude could cost them everything.

However, there is one entitlement we enjoy as Christians who spend our lifetimes faithfully following our Lord and Savior. We read in John 1:12 that "to all who did receive Him, to those who believed in His name, He gave the right to become children of God." But this gift is really more of an inheritance than an entitlement. When we choose to follow Jesus, eternal life is not something we are "inherently deserving of," as the true definition of the word *entitlement* suggests. Only by grace, when we come to Jesus, can we receive it. We must, in genuine humility, acknowledge His sovereignty, confess our sins, and receive redemption to join equally with other believers in the splendor of the life to come.

⌐═╼⊖

Keys to Kingdom Living: In God's economy, subservience supersedes entitlement.
Doorpost: "For everyone who exalts himself will be humbled, but he who humbles himself will be exalted." Luke 14:11 (ESV)

THE TRAP DOOR: HEDONISM

*H*ollywood and literature love to take a sow's ear and turn it into a silk purse. They often specialize in legitimizing the immoral and the illegal. You are no doubt familiar with compelling stories of poor unfortunates being faced with impossible choices that lead them to commit crimes that appear justified somehow. The terminally ill dad with four kids needs to leave a nest egg for his needy family, so he becomes a meth dealer. A widowed mother of two begins selling marijuana illegally to make ends meet. The wife of a wealthy, infirmed older man is given his permission to take a lover so she doesn't miss out on the sexual pleasures of youth. A young merry outlaw from Sherwood Forest robs the rich to give to the poor to balance socioeconomic inequity.

We sympathize with such characters and are drawn into their dilemmas, even though their behavior and actions are inherently wrong. What they exhibit is a form of justifiable hedonism. But the Enemy has a larger agenda at play: by making such actions appear as last resorts in losing scenarios, wrongdoings are not only legitimized, they are actually championed. He doesn't want what happens in Vegas to stay only in Vegas. His goal is to cause every man and woman to stumble; the line between right and wrong becomes blurred, not only to the person drawing it but also to those observing it.

This phenomenon is reflected in what is known as *ethical*

hedonism. It's based on the idea that all people have the right to do everything in their power to achieve the greatest amount of pleasure possible for themselves. Of course, the problem with such thinking is that it leaves the judgment of right and wrong up to each individual. Not all individuals adhere to the absolute doctrine derived from the Ten Commandments. When ethics are formulated apart from God's law, a slippery slope results, and the margin for error rises significantly.

When we find ourselves trying to compartmentalize a choice that may seem legitimate under special circumstances, we fall prey to character corruption. We are in no position to reframe the law or manipulate it to suit our needs and desires, no matter how dire they are. In our pride, we may be tempted to cross that line. But we are reminded repeatedly not to add to God's words. In the Contemporary English Version, we are told in Proverbs 30:6 not to "change what God has said. He will correct you and show you that you are a liar."

In light of that verse, today's media darling may very well be tomorrow's Pinocchio, the wooden puppet with a penchant for lies. So whether the temptations of hedonism are subtly grounded in circumstantial justification, or whether they are more identifiable, as in cases of drug abuse, sexual addiction, gluttony, drunkenness, larceny, or excess acquisition—all are at odds with God and His Word. Are you? Have you been busy constructing elaborate plot lines in the script of your life? Or are you traveling on the path that God has set before you, confessing after a misstep and quickly realigning yourself with His shepherd staff? Hedonists chase rainbows, but Christians aim to know and follow the One responsible for making them.

⊥—⊶

Keys to Kingdom Living: Avoid the trap of indulgence and remain grounded in obedience.

Doorpost: "You've already put in your time in that God-ignorant way of life . . . Now it's time to be done with it for good. Of course, your old friends don't understand why you don't join in with the old gang anymore. But you don't have to give an account to them. They're the ones who will be called on the carpet—and before God himself." I Peter 4:3-5 (MSG)

12

THE TRAP DOOR: HELPLESSNESS AND DEFEATISM

*A*s a woman "of a certain age," I lack a great deal of technological expertise. While it's true that I'm active on social media, I write using up-to-date software, and I use Square to sell books at appearances, I'm still a novice when it comes to tasks like using Snapchat and Canva. And I am completely terrified of electronic calendars! The latter may be more of a trust issue.

Sometimes, technology proves so overwhelming for me that it becomes a stumbling block. I must force myself to learn what is required for twenty-first-century daily living. Procrastination, dread, and defeatism sink into my spirit like a lead balloon, stifling my dreams like a gnarly hair clog in a bathtub drain. The only variable in this scenario involves how long I let the clog impede my progress. Pricilla Van Sutphin describes defeatism as "a stronghold of hopelessness binding one from being who God has made them to be."[1] When someone hacked into my website, I was unable to continue with my blog work; I was literally being bound from expressing myself the way God intended. Not knowing how to correct the problem initially, I allowed myself to be defeated by it. I was stuck.

The Enemy would love nothing more than to keep you ensnared in your trap of helplessness. He wants you to believe you can't do it, you won't make it, you're not good enough. In my case, I knew I was called to write, so I needed to find a way out of my helpless despair. Fortunately, I consulted God's Word, the spiritual Drano to any clogged drain du jour. I love what Romans 8:31 says about obstacles. "What, then, shall we say in response to these things? If God is for us, who can be against us?" Later, in verse 37, we see that "in all these things we are more than conquerors through Him who loved us."

As Christians, we are sometimes tempted to limit petitions to God only to family or spiritual matters, leaving Him out of boardrooms and workplaces. But God wants you to invite Him into every area of your life. In fact, Paul tells us in Colossians 3:23 that whatever we do, we should "work at it with all of [our] heart, as working for the Lord, not for human masters."

I remember feeling very helpless and defeated back in 1996, the day I was laid off from my assistant editor position at the *Los Angeles Times*. I was the assistant humor editor, a job I am sure looked quite easy to trim as the newspaper was facing another sale. My boss was out of town that day, and I had thought the night before that they would not have let him go out of town if they were going to let me go, because no one would be there to get the daily section out. But I was wrong. Through tears, I finished my work, even though my on-duty superiors told me I didn't have to. I wish I could tell you I was imagining Jesus' face as I completed my tasks, but that would be a lie. What I was doing was following through with my higher responsibility: completing the work initially entrusted to me. Feelings of helplessness and despair were immaterial. That's what Paul is saying here; our higher responsibility is to God, no matter what the task is.

Next time you are faced with a daunting task and feel like giving up, invite God into your dilemma. Tap into His wisdom, His strength, and His game plan. He'll help you spot the traps set before you. With His guidance, you can sail over potential pitfalls with newfound courage and renewed confidence.

⊢⸱⸱₿

Keys to Kingdom Living: God really is our ever-present help in times of perceived helplessness and defeat.
Doorpost: "I can do all things through Christ Jesus, who gives me strength." Philippians 4:13

THE TRAP DOOR: LAZINESS

*I*n one of my early jobs, I wrote advertising copy for a department store. Every copywriter had their own cubicle with a desk and a closet for hanging coats. One of my coworkers devised a daily scheme: after lunch, he would enter the closet for a nap, unbeknownst to his superiors. Of course, my fellow workers and I always knew what he was up to every day after lunch when he was nowhere to be found. Although on one level his ruse might appear somewhat comical, the fact is that his ritualized laziness cost the company money in light of his lack of productivity. To add insult to injury, he wasn't exactly a go-getter when he was awake! Today, the company is no longer in business. I'm not blaming my lazy former colleague for the demise of the store, but laziness does levy a cost, both for the person and their organization.

I've never considered myself to be a lazy person, but I've noticed as I get older that I do have some lazy tendencies. I have to fight against them. I don't always want to get out of my warm bed at dawn on a chilly morning for my quiet time with God. Or I put off running errands for my husband. Or I might give into laziness and listen to an online church broadcast. By not fully participating with my spiritual family on our modern-day Sabbath, I am not fully embracing the day. God originally intended the day to be set apart as holy and not lazy when He took the seventh day off Himself after creating the world.

Laziness—the failure to do what we are supposed to do, despite having the ability to do it—often stems from a bad attitude. This may spring from very real physical obstacles such as inactivity or poor nutrition, exhaustion or illness. Sometimes, emotional obstacles block our productivity. Lack of self-worth, for instance, can lead to indecisiveness, irresponsibility, distractibility, or a feeling of overwhelm that shuts you down completely. Everyone is prone to occasional bouts of laziness and leisurely pursuits. But if laziness becomes a predominate mindset, it can derail your goals and God's plan for your life.

Compared to other traps, laziness may seem benign to an outsider. But the Bible has plenty to say on the subject, and it's far from pretty. "If anyone is not willing to work, let him not eat," we read in 2 Thessalonians 3:10 (ESV). Harsher still is the admonition from Proverbs 13:9: "Whoever is slack in his work is a brother who destroys." And to the able-bodied but willfully idle who "know the right thing and fail to do it," as we read in James 4:17, they commit sin when they neglect to work. Indeed, we are to be fervent in spirit as we serve the Lord, not slothful in zeal, as we read in Romans 12:11 (ESV).

The key to combatting laziness is to fuel your motivation for proactivity. Surround yourself with Christian friends and mentors who are industrious, who take their callings and vocations seriously. Study edifying verses that fuel your motivation. Paul's letters to Titus, Timothy, and the Philippians and Galatians are filled with solid gems of wisdom about the merits of industrious pursuits. By filling your minds with the richness of these Scriptures, I pray that you and I will "spur one another on toward love and good deeds" (Hebrews 10:24). Our time on earth is limited compared to thousands of years in eternity. Until then, we need to roll up our sleeves and get to work.

⊢━⊖

Keys to Kingdom Living: Avoid the trap of laziness by filling your mind with motivational Scripture and your life with positive role models.

Doorpost: "The point is this: whoever sows sparingly will reap sparingly, and whoever sows bountifully will also reap bountifully." 2 Corinthians 9:6 (ESV)

WEEK 2: TWISTING

TWISTING: AWAY FROM GOD

a favorite restaurant of mine in Colorado ski country is called Twist. The name reflects the chefs' passion of fine cuisine reinvention. They pride themselves on taking a standard recipe and tweaking it just enough to christen an altogether newfangled dish. For example, instead of just serving standard spaghetti and meatballs, they start with homemade flat noodles and a Bolognese sauce, add roasted eggplant, and top it all off with meatballs made with mushrooms and quinoa.

The notion of twisting something involves a small but significant change. To twist something doesn't involve a 180-degree spin; it involves a smaller turn, which alters the original position as well as the perception. In our walk as Christians, if we do not stay positioned toward God, we can gradually find ourselves twisting away from Him. The twist might begin as something subtle. We trim out the study of God's Word from our schedule because we don't like the new teacher. Or perhaps we tolerate a behavior from our kids that runs counter to God's laws; we don't want to risk our relationship with them by standing up for God's agenda.

The problem with the twist is that, once we are going in one direction, we must mindfully turn the opposite way to correct the imbalance. Often, momentum in one direction is harder to correct once we have begun; we won't gravitate to a posture of holiness. This is why we are often compared to sheep in the

Bible. We need a shepherd to guide us back into the herd when we stray.

Without correction or intervention, an initial small twist away from God can tailspin into a marked separation. Thankfully, we can consult God's compass as we realign ourselves with His infallible navigation. We can rely on our great Navigator's comforting words to lost sojourner Thomas in John 14:5, where Jesus says, "I am the way and the truth and the life. No one comes to the Father except through me." If Jesus is the way, we can't afford not to correct our inevitable twists. If we stay rooted in God's Word, we will know His way for us. And we will abide in His promises for eternal life through Him.

Inevitably, we will likely experience a lifetime of doing the twist. We will gravitate away and again back to God in a continuous dance. In our human nature, we will pull away from God, and in our desire to remain rooted in Him we should aim to accept correction and realignment. We can pray to stay in alignment ourselves and pray for those we know who are in desperate need of it. Most importantly, we can read, memorize, and fully trust in His promises, knowing how important it is to trust our Navigator.

<hr />

Keys to Kingdom Living: Guard against twists away from God, and accept the correction of any ill-conceived momentum.
Doorpost: "We all, like sheep, have gone astray, each of us has turned our own way." Isaiah 53:6

TWISTING: AWAY FROM HIS PLAN

*W*ho doesn't rejoice over the beautifully abundant seasons with God, when we feel close to Him, reasonably happy with our circumstances, and in harmony with His plans and purposes? Because it's likely our next challenge is probably just around the corner.

Out of our deep love for the Lord comes a desire to please Him and do what He asks us to do, at least in general. But there are times in our walk when He begins to make it clear He wants us to do something that is wildly out of our comfort zone. Jonah learned it well when he ignored God's plans for him to travel to a place of great need. He ended up in the stomach of a big fish.

I still remember the day I took my eighteen-month-old son to be tested for developmental delays by a team of educators. We exchanged verbal pleasantries, but most of what they said was white noise to me except for the words, "He probably has autism."

As my son and I walked out of the room and onto a grassy mound on that spring day, a cool breeze blew through my hair. The beauty of the day was in sharp contrast to the dark unknowns present in my tomorrows. Tears began flowing down my cheeks, and I suddenly stopped dead in my tracks when this chilling thought passed through my mind: *Let go of his hand and just walk away from him.* The dread of the responsibility of years of frustration and heartache over all that would not be washed over me like a tidal wave of nausea. Pangs of guilt from the hypocrisy of not caring whether or not I birthed my child were comingling with a dread that perhaps I'd be paying a higher price than I had ever imagined. Of course it was illogical, inconceivable, and illegal, and something I would never be able to bring myself to do, but in that millisecond, it was tempting.

I knew some of what would lie ahead in raising him. Temper tantrums, special schooling, substantial physical and academic challenges, as well as the death of thousands of dreams. Thankfully, the Lord filled me with the strength and courage to resist temptation that day, as well as several others throughout the course of his life to date. There have been countless times I wanted to throw up my hands and walk away from God's plan or amend it to meet my needs. Although God did not let me walk away from the burden, He does remind me every day to lay it down and lean on Him, and to lean on the handful of His servants who come alongside me every day to help me accomplish the plan God has laid out for my son and for me.

God stood by His Son in the same way when Jesus stood on top of a mountain and Satan tempted Him to jump off and end His life, as recorded in Matthew 4. He stands by you and me each day we face as part of His larger plan. While we're tempted to twist away from it, He graciously steers us back on course when we permit Him to guide and direct us. When we trust God in the big and small details of our lives, we can be sure that He knows better than we do how to best live out our days on this earth to accomplish His plans and purposes. As I trust Him, I know He will help me hold onto the hands he's entrusted to me, while He holds onto mine to see me to the end of my journey.

—⊶—

Keys to Kingdom Living: Resist amending God's plans and conform your will to His.
Doorpost: "But the plans of the Lord stand firm, the purposes of His heart through all generations." Psalm 33:11

TWISTING: IN ORDER TO MOVE
AGAINST OUR FEARS

*D*aredevil personalities displaying death-defying behaviors are all over YouTube. They climb New York skyscrapers. Others jump rows of cars on motorcycles. Some join fellow thrill-seekers by bungee jumping, climbing Mount Everest, or skydiving out of airplanes.

But conquering fear continues to challenge the average person. Me, I can't even bring myself to risk parking in a twenty-minute spot if I might be half an hour in the store! Some of the healthier fears—don't drink tap water in Mexico, for instance—may serve you well in your lifetime. But daily living does require managing some risks.

We need to use our good judgment—and look to our Wise Counselor—as we examine, weigh, and ultimately choose whether or not to take a risk and move against a fear. Some common risks Christians face: traveling to nonsecure destinations to deliver the good news, trusting Him with finances through tithing ten percent of "first fruit" income, and going out on a limb to witness to a friend and facing possible rejection.

Many Bible verses speak to the rewards on the flip side of these risks. In Isaiah 52:7 we read, "How beautiful on the mountains are the feet of those who bring good news." In Proverbs 3:9-10 we read, "Honor the Lord with your wealth and with the first fruits of all your produce; then your barns will be filled with plenty and your vats will be bursting with wine"

(ESV). And in Acts 20:24, Paul says he considers his life to be worth nothing, with his only aim "to finish the race and complete the task the Lord Jesus has given [him]—the task of testifying to the good news of God's grace."

If we don't put our fears in check, we become paralyzed. When we don't move at all, we are ineffective workers in the kingdom force. We ignore passions and fail to accomplish our purposes. But when we pray for guidance, heed God's direction, and move against fear, we plug into God's power to go the distance. When we enlist His help, we often find that the fear turns out to be far less significant than we imagined.

I remember the first time I climbed onto the balance beam in gym class. We had to do a backwards cartwheel, which required literal blind faith, and land on the narrow board with both feet. This task seemed impossible to me, but my teacher promised to spot me. She held her hands under the small of my back for added support. I pulled it off—though, truth be told, I'm no Simone Biles! Thankfully, when we look to God for support, we can blindly trust that He will help us, as well.

⸻

Keys to Kingdom Living: Pray for courage and strength to move against your fears to go the distance.
Doorpost: "So do not fear, for I am with you; do not be dismayed, for I am your God. I will strengthen you and help you. I will uphold you with my righteous right hand." Isaiah 41:10

TWISTING: GOD'S VERY WORD

*P*oliticians are famous for manipulating language to dodge reporters' questions, get their all-important points across, and place their agendas before the public at all costs. As anyone who has ever been interviewed knows, it's easy to pontificate on a variety of topics if the speaker has enough finesse and charm to effectively distract their audience. Children can often bring this skill to the table as they try to avoid talking about upcoming tests, grades, or other potentially controversial subjects by diverting parents to off-topic talk.

This kind of spin also occurs when people assemble to talk about God's law in light of the modern age—this age of supposed tolerance and "fresh morality." There are those who question the relevance of some of God's laws. To their mind, some of what is found on those ancient pages is out of touch and shouldn't necessarily be upheld as relevant today.

When individuals begin to sift through the whole of God's truth to try to separate what they find acceptable in their minds from what they don't, they place their own discernment over God's. As a result, they put the god of their own wisdom before the one true God, breaking the first commandment in the process. Much is found in Scripture discouraging this dangerous activity. In James 2:10 we read that "whoever keeps the whole law but fails in one point will be accountable for all of it" (NET). We are not given free rein to pick and choose what to obey based on our personal comfort zones or carefully constructed compartments.

It's made very clear in 2 Timothy 3:16 that "all scripture is breathed out by God and useful for teaching, reproof, correction, and training in righteousness" (ESV). The word "all" cannot be translated to "some." We cannot dismiss the story of creation or the virgin birth as "not God-breathed," because it *is* in the Scriptures and must be embraced rather than replaced. Man's laws—or popular thinking—must never take precedence over God's laws. In Acts 5:27, we saw that the apostles appeared before the high priests who had warned them not to preach in the name of Jesus. Their response to them was simply this: "We must obey God rather than human beings."

Human authority pales in comparison to God's. In Matthew 28:18, Jesus makes it clear who it is that really rules and reigns, saying, "All authority in heaven and on earth has been given to me." When we try to alter His words based on our whims, we are willfully disobeying God's laws and will ultimately pay a high price for it.

<hr>

Keys to Kingdom Living: Revere God's Word in its entirety and avoid altering it.

Doorpost: "If anyone teaches a different doctrine and does not agree with the sound words of our Lord Jesus Christ and the teaching that accords with godliness, he is puffed up with conceit and understands nothing." 1 Timothy 6:3 (ESV)

TWISTING: TO ADJUST TO HARSH CIRCUMSTANCES WITH GRACE

*In 2011, I had the privilege of getting to know a high school freshman named Jake Olson. This amazing young man lost his left eye at ten months old to a rare form of retinal cancer. His cancer returned eight times, and by the time he was twelve, he lost his right eye as well and became totally blind. Though he acknowledges there were some initial setbacks from these challenging obstacles, he demonstrated tremendous courage and developed a game plan to overcome the obstacles that stood in his way. As a result, he's accomplished more than many typical young men his age.

He played high school golf with the help of his service dog and a loving father who helped him line up the ball. He made the football team at the University of Southern California as a long snapper. His book, *Open Your Eyes: 10 Uncommon Lessons to Discover a Happier Life*, is rich with divine inspiration on how God really does "work for the good of those who love him, who have been called according to his purposes," as He promises in Romans 8:28.

He recently told a newspaper reporter that he wanted to be recognized after he leaves this earth as a man who defined his circumstances instead of letting his circumstances define him. Ask anyone who knows Jake Olson and he or she will tell you he's all about encouraging, dreaming big, and giving God the glory.

Do we confine our circumstances to the margins, or do they occupy center stage in our lives? If we are honest in our answer, we probably do a little bit of both. But we can strive to toss them to the margins as Jesus did. He was born to die and to "give His life as a ransom for many," as He said in Mark 10:45. But He didn't walk around bemoaning His fate. Instead He devoted His life to bringing redemption, grace, and salvation to a fallen world and spreading the hope and joy it would bring to others.

That's exactly what we need to be doing. We need to rise above our circumstances. It's a God-sized task we can only do with His help, but it's essential in our daily walk with God for two important reasons: it helps us fully rely on God, no matter what is going on in our lives, and it serves as a model for others when they can see the hope and joy we have, despite the problems we face day to day. People are watching.

—•₿

Keys to Kingdom Living: Minimize the impact of your circumstances and maximize God's impact in diminishing their significance as an overcomer and example to others.

Doorpost: "I have learned the secret of being content in any and every situation, whether well fed or hungry, whether living in plenty or in want. I can do all this through Him who gives me strength." Philippians 4:12-13

TWISTING: TO THE LEFT TO HELP
THE UNSAVED

I'm guilty of selective vision. If I'm in the middle of the grocery store and I see someone I know will want to engage in a lengthy conversation with me, I sometimes hide behind the produce island. Or if I'm going inside the coffee shop, I don't always make eye contact with the man at the foot of the door holding the sign asking for money. From time to time, we all put on our horse blinders to block out what is inconvenient to address. We keep our body moving forward, trying not to divert from that day's plan of action.

But just because a pile of radicchio obscures our eyes from the eyes of those who might need us, that doesn't mean we're not on the hook for a missed opportunity. Our vegetable hide-and-seek stunt may have prevented a divine appointment. We might have been able to encourage or simply give a warm hug to someone who had been alone all day without speaking to a single soul. These gestures are particularly important when it comes to people to whom we can show genuine love and care, or those who are unsaved.

When God deems it time, He will call His "sheep," His beloved believers, to His right, and the "goats," those not guided into the pen of the redeemed, to His left. Like most if not all of those who read this, I want *all* my loved ones, friends, and even casual acquaintances to be with me in the herd on the right. So, like you, I need to make a point of twisting to the left to try—with the Holy Spirit's help—to initiate the crossover.

We need to be ready, willing, and eager, long before an opportunity arises. The best way to do this is to cultivate an attitude of surrender and the laying down of our rights. We need to put others first. I remember as a young mother, right after we brought our first son home, I would struggle with what the morning would look like for me after thirty-eight years of caring primarily for myself. I imagined the perfect morning of getting Ben Alex fed, followed by his first long nap, during which I would drink my hot coffee, eat a hot breakfast, read the entire morning paper, and get dinner prepped and the house tidied up before he awoke so we could spend the afternoon playing. Anyone who's even watched a baby knows they work on their own timetable, not yours! It wasn't long until submission to his schedule and his needs became my reality.

Looking back on those days now, I wouldn't trade one second of those little daily surrender moments for the hot coffee or the forgettable news updates. Investing in people counts for the kingdom. The mom of five kids who lives next door that you just met and the pregnant woman at the gas station trying to scrape money together for a night in a motel need you. When you forgo your proverbial hot coffee scenario, you are putting their needs before yours, just as Jesus would do.

⌐•❧

Keys to Kingdom Living: Abandon your straight-ahead agenda and twist to the left to bring others over to His right.
Doorpost: "Resist the devil, and he will flee from you." James 4:7

TWISTING: TO THE RIGHT TO HELP
ENCOURAGE THE SHEEP

*I*t's often said in the Christian community that the spiritual gift of encouragement is underused in churches today. Yet few obstacles stand in the way of its practice. It requires no monetary investment. It doesn't depend on intelligence, social station, popularity, or the appearance of the one who delivers it.

Genuine encouragement simply requires a singular motivation: to help enable someone. It might be for the purpose of helping them overcome a seemingly impossible problem or situation. Or it may be to aid them in recognizing, cultivating, nurturing, and ultimately using their gifts and talents. Either way, the recipient is always blessed when the Christian encourager takes the time to tend to his or her brothers and sisters.

Sometimes we're so busy keeping an eye on lost sheep that we forget about the care of the ones in our "pen." But those in our pen whom we are entrusted to love readily discern the difference. They know the difference between a warm body that brushes past them and the one they can call at three in the morning when a crisis unfolds. American optimist William Arthur Ward once wrote, "Flatter me, and I may not believe you. Criticize me, and I may not like you. Ignore me, and I may not forgive you. Encourage me, and I will not forget you."[1]

The Holy Spirit is our ready resource for lighting up those little leadings to send someone a card, offer a compliment, or come alongside with a little hug and an offer of prayer. Next time that spark of an idea goes off in your head, don't ignore it or jot it on a forgettable to-do list. Just do it! We don't need to fret about the potential success or impact. All we need to do is listen to the Holy Spirit and act.

I recently had such a leading. A Christian friend of mine was moving cross-country to a place where she didn't know a soul. When she shared that she was nervous about making new friends, I suggested she check out the local class of a non-denominational Bible study I've been in for years. Knowing she had a long to-do list herself, I looked up the info and texted it to her.

A few weeks later, she texted me back to say that she enrolled, was very excited, and thanked me for suggesting it. Because I made the effort without procrastinating, she connected immediately. There may come a day may come when she meets someone and prompts them to join her at the same study. One person makes an impact. That impact is the catalyst encouraging someone else. And there's an added bonus besides just helping someone else. Chances are, your sincere efforts will be much appreciated by others as well, and you'll delight in knowing that God is glorified in the process.

—⊶⊱—

Keys to Kingdom Living: Help tend the Good Shepherd's flock with encouragement.
Doorpost: "And let us consider how we may spur one another towards love and good deeds." Hebrews 10:24

WEEK 3: ABANDON

ABANDON: IGNORING OUR AGENDA
TO CLING TO HIS

*I*f your to-do list is anything like mine, on it you have short-term items that will be crossed off in a few days as well as long-term items that you've been putting off since the new millennium. If only we could slice ourselves to delegate the non-desirable tasks to another half. I remember a young expectant mom once confessing she was concerned about the "drudgery tasks" of motherhood, admitting she preferred arranging flowers over kitchen cleanup. I have often wondered how she ended up faring with the inevitable vomit and potty duties she had no idea she was facing.

Any parent reading this will likely concede that the work of motherhood is worth the sacrifices in light of the outcome: raising someone who you'd likely lay down your life for, and in many ways already have. Recent statistics show the average cost of raising a child born in 2015 will come to between $233K and $284K, according to a CNN statistic.[1] With a comfortable trip around the world costing about $40,000, a person could make that journey about seven times with the same amount of money, according to the A Little Adrift travel newsletter.[2] I would imagine that if a parent could go back in time and had the ability to reverse parenthood, few would opt out, and most would concur that all the sacrifices were worth it.

That is surely how God felt when He sacrificed His Son for you and me and the billions of other people who've lived and died and are yet to be born. Love prompted God to create Adam and Eve. Love prompted Him to design a plan for redemption that cost Him dearly. Authentic allegiance to God also comes at a cost. We are called to abandon our old way of life and surrender to His will for our lives.

The word *abandon* means to completely give up a course of action, a practice, or a way of thinking. When we become Christians, we give up relying on our own will for our lives as the sole deciding factor of our decisions. The practice of doing whatever we want, and in the timing and manner we choose, is ideally replaced with His divine intervention. Our way of thinking is transformed by our minds being renewed, as we read in Romans 12:2. We are, indeed, no longer conformed to the pattern of this world; the idea of ourselves as deities that's so popular in our culture becomes dead in the water as Jesus navigates our course and captains our ship.

Anyone who's ever embraced a goal God had for them that required sacrifice knows the intrinsic rewards. Mother Teresa gave up her affluent life as an eighteen-year-old in the Balkans to begin her service to God in Ireland, eventually landing in Calcutta. There, she served the poorest of the poor for the rest of her earthly life. She once said, "A sacrifice to be real must cost, must hurt, and must empty ourselves."[3] How very true!

Keys to Kingdom Living: Abandoning our goals and giving birth to God's goals can bring us joy.

Doorpost: "For whoever wants to save their life will lose it, but whoever loses their life for me will find it." Luke 9:24

ABANDON: DISCERNING WHAT TO DITCH AND WHAT TO KEEP

*M*y desk is full of a variety of items, from the vital to the trivial. My desktop computer and pens are obviously important tools. Pictures of my family might seem trivial, but to me they are a must. One could argue that the five scented candles on my desk are not necessities—but when I light them, it creates a nice ambience for my workspace. The Eiffel Tower sculpture tucked away in the corner is for sure something I could ditch, but I enjoy it and would be hard pressed to remove it.

The gulf between *need* and *want* is substantial, except when it comes to the eye of the beholder. A five-year-old staring at his Christmas list deems his number one item as a need, not a want. On his sixteenth birthday, a teenager might see a car as a need, but the parent staring at the insurance quote for him may be inclined to disagree. The same blind spots occur when we look at our schedules. We cannot let everything stay on our desks. What would Marie Kondo say if she popped over for tea and organizing?

Even some good things will need to be trimmed off the schedule. For instance, I know a woman who attends a large non-denominational Bible study, as well as another she runs at her church, and yet another for couples. Even she concedes it's too much for her schedule. We need to truly examine the amount of time we have and ask God to help us discern what we should keep on the calendar and what we should say no to.

I recently heard a sermon that delineated four basic categories of to-do lists. They included (1) the things God wants me to do, (2) the things I need to do for loved ones, (3) the things I want to do, and (4) the things others want me to do. These categories are listed in the order they were important to the speaker, and I agree that it is an appropriate hierarchy. When Jesus stayed at the temple three days after His parents departed, as recorded in Luke 2, He followed his leading from God to remain there (Category 1) even though it conflicted with his parents' plans (Category 2).

The very best outcome is when Category 1 and Category 3 are the same—but it won't always be so. Sometimes we don't feel like cracking open our Bible. We may be tempted to stay in bed on a cold morning with the covers pulled over our heads. But truth be told, we are always blessed when we do what God wants us to do, regardless of our desires or feelings. But when it comes to Category 4, we should always use the measuring stick of whether God really wants us to do it. More importantly, are we just doing something out of obligation to someone else as a people-pleasing exercise? Obligatory surrender doesn't really serve any other purpose in the final analysis. I was once asked to serve on a financial committee at my church. I am not gifted in this area and am terrible with numbers. But I said *yes* out of obligation . . . and I did not serve on it long, as a result. By prioritizing our schedule and following what He matches our gifts to, we effectively manage our time for God.

— ⚭

Keys to Kingdom Living: Careful prioritizing and seeking the Holy Spirit's guidance keeps us focused on His agenda for us.

Doorpost: "Walk in wisdom towards outsiders, making the best use of the time." Colossians 4:5 (ESV)

ABANDON: GIVING UP A NEST OF EAGLES TO WELCOME BABY BIRDS

*Y*ou may have heard someone say that you can't soar with the eagles if you're running with the turkeys. While it's true that we want to surround ourselves with people who can bring us up higher, we must allow ourselves to be that person for someone else. This requires a delicate balance in forming alliances in which both of these processes can flourish.

In befriending those we are trying to help, boundaries must be put into place and honored. We must first recognize our own limitations and be solidly rooted before helping others out of the same struggle. If you are a recently recovered gambler, you might want to avoid hanging out in casinos with others who struggle with it too, even if your goal is to bring them up higher. It's a good idea to strike a balance between the turkeys and eagles, making sure you have a solid number of eagles that is not disproportionate to the number of turkeys, even if today's turkeys may turn out to be tomorrow's swans! According to the *Huffington Post*, statistics show that we are the average of the five people we hang out with the most[1]—something to think about in the larger scheme of things.

One big concern we need to weigh as we befriend the lost, or even offer wise counsel to a fellow Christian, is that of standing for the truth in love. When people mess up, we need to be there to support them and remind them of God's forgiveness.

When a godly person is struggling with a situation and is tempted to do something running contrary to God's Word, we can't just agree with them out of convenience and friendship. An authentic relationship requires honesty and accountability to what God's Word says, all delivered in love, without malice, condemnation, or judgment on our part.

Sometimes in this scenario when we're the ones struggling, we must be open to the wise counsel others are giving us. We must put aside any arrogance and admit our infallibility. No one is above reproach this side of eternity. The truth is, we rarely have the perspective we need to completely evaluate our own situations objectively. That is why we need other Christians' advice just as much as they need ours when it's God-driven and inspired. In Proverbs 12:15 we read, "The way of a fool is right in his own eyes, but a wise man listens to advice" (ESV). Seeking more than once source is also helpful, as we read in Proverbs 11:14: "Where there is no guidance, a people fails, but in an abundance of counselors there is safety" (ESV).

Surrounding ourselves with only eagles isn't the right approach either. Jesus befriended the marginalized—it was His mission. But He also surrounded Himself with his twelve disciples who supported Him in his work, providing a model for teamwork ministry that continues to inspire today.

⌐━●

Keys to Kingdom Living: Balance your time with those who need you and the companions *you* need.

Doorpost: "Do not carouse with drunkards or feast with gluttons, for they are on their way to poverty, and too much sleep clothes them in rags." Proverbs 23:20-21 (NLT)

ABANDON: DISCERNING WHEN
LOYALTY IS APPROPRIATE

*o say that relationships can be difficult is a huge understatement. In Woody Allen's *Annie Hall*, the main character retells an old joke and ends it with a telling observation.

> "This guy goes to a psychiatrist and says, 'Doc, my brother's crazy! He thinks he's a chicken.' The doctor says 'Well, why don't you turn him in?' Then the guy says, 'I would, but I need the eggs . . .' I guess that's pretty much how I feel about relationships. They're totally irrational, and crazy, and absurd, but I guess we keep going through it because most of us 'need the eggs.'"

We are born with a God-shaped hole in our hearts and are wired for a variety of relationships—friendly, romantic, and work-related. God Himself said in Genesis 2:18 that it is not good for man to live alone. But sometimes *alone* looks good to us. The compromises, sacrifices, and accommodations we need to make for others feel exhausting. There's nothing wrong with stealing away for a little solitude now and then, but when we are tempted to throw out perfectly good relationships because of inconvenience or misunderstanding, that's when we need a motive check.

The Enemy loves to isolate, conquer, and divide us. He will work within our minds to distort, skew, and alter misunderstandings or minor issues into something major. This is something I personally have to safeguard because I tend to blow things out of proportion and often need to be talked down off the ledge. The old saying about throwing out the baby with the bathwater is something I need to guard against. When I am tempted to write someone off, I try to examine what my true motives are and more often than not realize I had myself in knots for imaginary reasons.

I once found myself in a situation where I felt I needed to sever a friendship, so I did. A friend with an alcohol problem was getting herself deeper and deeper into all kinds of moral and even legal trouble. She fabricated a fraudulent lawsuit, lost her home, and eventually spent most of her waking hours hanging out in bars. The last time I talked to her, she basically confessed to me that she enjoyed her hedonistic lifestyle and had absolutely no interest in changing it. There was simply nowhere for our friendship to go.

Self-protection is probably the most viable reason to end a friendship or relationship. If, after setting healthy boundaries with a toxic person, that person continues to abuse, criticize, threaten, or even harm you, it's time to sever ties. But this should be a rare exception as we learn to live and love, offering forgiveness and understanding whenever possible.

⊢—⊷

Keys to Kingdom Living: Sever ties as a last resort when keeping the peace comes at too high a cost.
Doorpost: "A man of many companions may come to ruin, but there is a friend who sticks closer than a brother." Proverbs 18:24 (ESV)

ABANDON: LETTING GO—LEAVING
AND BEING LEFT

s hard as it sometimes is to sever relationships, no one likes to be the one left behind, either. In this life we are going to face instances where we are misunderstood or cast aside for a variety of reasons. Some of these instances will make sense to us and others will not. In some cases, I believe God protects us from various dangers and pitfalls by ending some relationships for us. I certainly find this to be true in relation to my search for a mate and how God spared me from some less-than-ideal selections, had I been entirely left to my own devices. Thankfully, I dodged some potentially lethal bullets here and there, but I digress.

For a while in college, I hung out with a rough crowd. This group of students was international, and I enjoyed being around their cultural differences. Then one day I had an epiphany: some of the group's activities I witnessed were getting so far out of hand that I made a conscious decision not to keep company with them anymore. I felt a little guilty about the choice, but about a month later, acquaintances of those individuals were arrested. Thankfully, I have been able to restore some of those relationships, now that time and life-saving conversions have occurred as they embraced spirituality and redemption in their own lives.

I've been misunderstood and cast aside as well—without restoration. Not being invited to a party while seeing photos of the event on Facebook can whittle away at my emotional well-being, if I choose to let it. I have to consciously work on perspective and importance in order to protect my heart from needless beatings that have more to do with my imagination than the reality of a situation.

Once, a good friend invited my husband and me to her dad's house for a party. I'd never been there—this was pre-cell phone and navigation. Hubby and I, map in hand, set out but could not find it on our old map. We stopped and called and got further directions but were still unable to find it after more than an hour. Rather than bothering them during the party, we simply gave up. When I called her the next day to explain, she accused me of lying about the map. She threw out twelve years of friendship for a lie she chose to believe. We need to take care that we aren't jumping to conclusions when it comes to severing ties. Recently, I tried to contact her but was again rebuffed; time to let it go, for sure.

When we discern that our relationship with Jesus Christ must stand at the top of our relational pyramid, we realize that all our other relationships will pale in comparison. Furthermore, any of our relationships with like-minded Christians will enjoy a higher level of satisfaction and purpose because of shared core values. By concentrating on the wealth of friendships blessed and provided by God, we can more readily accept the ones that deteriorate. We need to pray for perspective to accept those losses more gracefully.

⊶⊶

Keys to Kingdom Living: Accept the ebb and flow of friendships.
Doorpost: "A righteous man is cautious in friendship." Proverbs 12:26 (BSB)

ABANDON: BEING ALL IN FOR GOD

I remember the early days of my firstborn son's life and the degree to which my husband and I abandoned all other aspects of daily life to fully devote ourselves to his needs. Heightened states of cleanliness were a priority. Simplified evening meals made way for multiple bottle feedings. During his first month of life, I'm almost certain I took a picture of him every day, wanting to capture the smallest of changes. My husband even took to warming his little crib with a heating pad to make nighttime snuggling in his swaddling blanket an even more inviting prospect.

Babies for sure have a way of taking over a household, but eager parents usually yield to the process with a unique hybrid of sacrificial joy. After all, months, if not years, have been spent waiting for the little bundle to arrive. The same kind of enthusiasm occurs when a new love blossoms. The two beloveds long one for the other with a newfound intensity that can rarely sustain itself for any prolonged length of time.

Sustaining that kind of abandon in our relationship with God is even more challenging, especially for the mature Christian. For those who had the "aha" moment and can record the day and time of their conversion, remembering that mountaintop moment enables them to tap into that zeal. But for those who grew up in the faith, the zenith of their journey might be harder to chronicle. I prefer to liken my own walk with God to the action of magnet to metal. I remember singing songs of Jesus and His love as a young child, which began a slow journey towards the "metal"—namely, God Himself. As I grew older and life's hard knocks began to batter me around a bit, I would move closer but would stall out—not exactly moving away, but not thrusting forward at light speed, either.

During a particularly tough time in my life, I found myself in a position where leaning on Jesus was the only thing that made sense. I began to center my life, focusing on learning and experiencing the things of God in a way I never had before. It was at this point that my inner "magnet" began sprinting to its target, with a substantial push from the Holy Spirit. These days, I know I am securely attached to Him. And even on the days when I may not feel this, I remind myself that I still am. He promises His flock in John 10:29 that "no one can snatch them out of my Father's hand." We can take this promise to the bank!

Our emotion-driven culture entices us to base relationships on sheer feelings alone. But by continually reviewing His promises and bathing ourselves in His Word, we fuel the fire first ignited by the Holy Spirit. When we practice the arts of worship and praise, we honor God as well as remind ourselves of His awesome love for us. The resulting joy serves us well and also attracts others to His enriching salt and marvelous light.

Keys to Kingdom Living: Renew your abandon to God by bathing yourself in His presence.
Doorpost: "Never be lacking in zeal, but keep your spiritual fervor, serving the Lord." Romans 12:11

ABANDON: WHAT GOD NEVER DOES

As a child, I loved looking at illustrations of Jesus with sheep and children nestled in His lap. Images of Jesus taking care of little ones are popular in Sunday school art, as are little "visits with God" books, because children know they need looking after. But because my basic emotional and physical needs were met as a child, I didn't fully internalize the role of Good Shepherd in my life until I was much older.

As losses, disappointments, and realized fears began to mount in my life—namely, infertility and depression—I recognized my deep and profound need to internalize God's peace and providence in my life. The arrogant, imagined invincibility of my youth in many ways obstructed my need for God. He is completely devoted to us in ways no human being will ever be capable of doing. The longer I live, the more I realize that human love is not infallible, even if it is well-intended, fully committed, and freely offered. This is true about the love I receive as well as the love I give.

Reading the book *A Shepherd Looks at Psalm 23* by W. Phillip Keller helped me crystalize these attributes of God. Keller outlines the various characteristics of a shepherd—compassion, sacrifice, guidance, and love, to name a few. A former shepherd himself, Keller compares God's caretaking to real life shepherding. We have a saying in our family that we can't do buffets because we are like farm animals, meaning we can't be left to our own devices when it comes to eating. Most people are naturally more inclined toward self-indulgence than they are to holiness. Keller points out that the tipped-over sheep cannot right itself, and it needs the shepherd's intervention to set itself on its feet. Keller's examination of the simplistic and utterly dependent nature of the sheep themselves may be hard to admit to, but it is accurate.

Other leaders besides Christ may appear to be "shepherd-like" . . . but they aren't, pointing to the reason why transferring trust to someone other than the Good Shepherd has catastrophic consequences. Yet in life we often place total trust in a person or thing—a boyfriend, a clique of friends, a career, or an amassed life savings—only to see how mislaid it was. The Good Shepherd description embodies a loving portrait of God and His protected forever family. We are prone to dangers seen and unseen in this world. We need the trustworthy wisdom and foolproof guidance of our Good Shepherd.

By far, the most important thing we learn about the Good Shepherd is that He is unmatched in His willingness to sacrifice His very self. In John 10:11 we read, "I am the good shepherd: the good shepherd lays down His life for the sheep." No matter what happens in this life, He won't abandon those who put their trust in Him. Such inimitable faithfulness is a hallmark of the amazing God we love and serve.

━━⊱

Keys to Kingdom Living: Count on God; He's your anchor for life and beyond.
Doorpost: "The Lord himself goes before you and will be with you. He will never leave you or forsake you." Deuteronomy 31:8

WEEK 4: INJUSTICE

INJUSTICE: RECONCILING INJUSTICE IN OUR WORLD

*A*s a former newspaper journalist, I'm obsessed with keeping abreast of current events. I was in a newsroom when the Challenger exploded in 1986 and again in 1995 when the Oklahoma City bombing incident occurred. Newsmakers are naturally inclined to check for headlines and keep news radio stations on throughout the day. But I have tried to make it a point in recent years not to begin reading the paper until I have entered the Lord's presence and been reminded of His Good News that never changes, always encourages, and gives us the hope we need every day of our lives. I do this to begin the day with meaningful priority and also to protect my mind and heart from undue distress.

We don't need to look far to be reminded of the injustice and evil that permeates our world today. Terrorism, human trafficking, corporate theft and greed, political corruption, domestic violence, the rise of cults and the occult, and fractured family life are just a few of the problems we face in the twenty-first century. Images and headlines pop up on our phones, desktops, radios, and TVs. While we need to be aware of the world's problems (and, to some degree, be a part of the solution rather than the problem), we don't need to immerse and enmesh ourselves in them. We need to be in the world but not of it (John 17:16) in both our active life and our thought life.

After my parents retired, for the most part, their TV

remained tuned to the news channel from morning to night. I think by doing this, my mom and dad felt like they would know what was going on in any given moment. While I understand this desire, I noticed that over time there was a shift in their mentality. Though they probably were unaware of it, their anxiety level heightened, and their glass, once half full, deteriorated to half-empty status. The Bible tells us in Philippians 4:8 that "whatever is true, whatever is noble, whatever is right, whatever is pure, whatever is lovely, whatever is admirable—if anything is excellent or praiseworthy—think about such things."

Some of you might read that and think, well, that's fine for the *super* Christian, but I live in the real world and I'm not going to bury my head in the sand. Such a response is understandable, but I believe we need to strike a balance. We need to cultivate a compromise between not knowing what is going on versus obsessing day and night about what a terrible world we live in. We should not be afraid to venture beyond our doorsteps. God gave us encouraging promises for a reason. It's important to remind ourselves of them so we remember that no matter what happens, our names are in the Book of Life and absolutely nothing can snatch us out of His protective hand (John 10:28).

⌐━⬦

Keys to Kingdom Living: Trusting God and His promises and remaining in His Word will help us cope with the myriad horrors of global injustice.

Doorpost: "In the world you'll have trouble, but be courageous—I've overcome the world." John 16:33 (NET)

INJUSTICE: FRAMING UNFAIRNESS
FOR OUR CHILDREN

The expression of a child who has come face-to-face with injustice is among the saddest things a parent can view. I remember my son's face as he saw the television images of a plane flying directly into the World Trade Center building on 9/11. Fortunately, it occurred to me to turn the television off immediately after he saw it once so he would not be faced with the memory of repeated images of what happened. He was only five at the time. I was four when President Kennedy was shot, yet the television remained on in our Dallas home. I'm not saying I was scarred, but I do have a vague memory of the images of that day.

Our job as parents is to make our children feel safe and loved. Of course we know, sadly, that many children in this broken world don't feel safe or loved. Some don't have other basic needs met. Because children have a limited ability to put things into perspective, there is a danger of global issues being blown out of proportion. There is a famous scene in Woody Allen's movie *Annie Hall* in which the childhood version of Allen's character stops doing his homework and won't eat. His mother explains to a therapist that the boy is obsessed with the idea that "the universe is expanding." The therapist gently explains to the boy that he should simply enjoy himself while he can, adding that the final expansion won't happen for many years to come.

This funny scene of that young boy taking science so seriously bears out an important point: kids often blow fears out of proportion. We can teach our kids at an early age to pray to God when they are afraid as we comfort them with a loving touch, a hug, or other compassionate interventions. We can regularly tuck them into warm beds, pray with them, kiss them goodnight, and encourage them to sleep without fear until the morning sun peeks into their rooms.

But when our kids begin to learn about kidnappings, murders, and other injustices committed by evil people, we are confronted with the unpleasant task of explaining, and framing, these sad realities for them. We must convey the truth that the majority of adults they'll encounter in life will be trustworthy and not warrant fear or suspicion. Yet others will be wolves disguised in sheep's clothing. We must pray for our discernment as well as for theirs. We must pray for recognition of evil and to be delivered from it, as we read in Matthew 6:13 at the end of the Lord's Prayer.

Finally, we can model the ability to cope with injustice to our children by showing how to exercise sensible caution. We can avoid letting fear and anxiety entrap our mindsets. For instance, we can lock our doors and maybe set an alarm, as opposed to, say, hiring security guards or a bodyguard. We want them to see us being careful without overreacting, all the while reminding them of our trust in God.

———⚷

Keys to Kingdom Living: Seek God's wisdom as you frame world concerns for your kids.
Doorpost: "You shall teach [God's Word] diligently to your children, and shall talk of [it] when you sit in your house, and when you walk by the way, and when you lie down and when you rise." Deuteronomy 6:6-7 (BSB)

INJUSTICE: MANAGING THE STING OF PERSONAL INJUSTICES

*S*ometime in between childhood and old age, anyone living on the face of the earth will face personal injustice. These inequities stem from a variety of sources—some expected, and others out of the blue. In the '90s, I applied for a job as a fashion editor and found myself among the top contenders. The person who would be my editor if I was to get the job was very encouraging during interviews with upper management, but when it came to the final decision, he called to tell me that I wouldn't be hired. He hinted that the reason in part was that I wasn't a member of a minority, while another less experienced woman was. She prevailed, even though it wasn't his choice. Fair? Not to my mind, but that's the way the cookie crumbles.

We have all probably felt the sting of small injustices in our lives. Perhaps we've been slighted by hostesses who neglected to invite us to their parties, or we've been maligned by untrue gossip. Maybe we've experienced random vandalism or are unsuspectingly overcharged for goods or services. Sometimes larger, immense injustices, like being targeted for a hate crime or enduring the cruel horror of a loved one being murdered, bring about a more vilified response from individuals who were similarly victimized.

The size of the injustice is of lesser consequence to the one who must bear it. When we face unfairness, we have a hard time when we don't see the scales equaled before our very eyes. Of course, it's much easier to get past a party slight than it is to lose a child. Those two consequences don't even belong in the same sentence. Justice may sometimes be dispensed to the perpetrator via the judicial system, but when one life is lost at the fault of another, the scales are never fully balanced. Even if a criminal pays for a crime, full restitution this side of eternity can never fully be made.

Well-meaning, misguided, people may even insist that we "dust ourselves off" and move past our disappointment. I knew one woman who lost a daughter to a drunk driver. She was told at her church after less than six months had passed that she was wallowing in her loss, and it was ungodly on her part to keep dwelling on it! Thankfully, she did not internalize this ill-conceived response and instead found a more supportive community of believers.

The best way to endure injustice is to take our pain to God and ask Him to help us manage it. We trust in Jesus Christ as the only true and righteous Judge. He'll right wrongs for us. In John 5:22 we read, "The Father judges no one, but has entrusted all judgment to the Son." We may have to wait until the Day of Atonement when Christ comes again in glory, but God's timing is perfect—and as He promises in Romans 8:28, He'll use all things "for good for those who love God and are called according to His purpose" (ESV).

一·₿

Keys to Kingdom Living: Let Jesus balance your scale of injustice as only He can.
Doorpost: "O Lord of hosts, who judges righteously, who tries the feelings and the heart, let me see Your vengeance on them. For to you I have committed my cause." Jeremiah 11:19-20 (NASB)

INJUSTICE: HOW TO BATTLE
AGAINST IT

*O*ften when we think of injustice, we are more inclined to direct our thoughts to being victimized by it. But what about when we find ourselves perpetuating an injustice? If you're reading this devotion, you are probably sensitive to global injustice and can recognize mistreatment in others when you see it.

Recognizing this trait takes more effort. It isn't easy to admit, but because we are by nature sinful and unclean, we are guilty of injustice. We might be guilty of emotional favoritism with regard to a nephew, niece, or parent, and those feelings may result in unfair treatment of others involved. It might present itself in a small way—we might cut in line at an entertainment or sports venue, or edge in front of someone for a parking spot they were waiting for. We aren't trying to perpetuate injustice, but by putting our own needs ahead of what is fair, the outcome remains unfair.

Sometimes an injustice is buried deep in our hearts, minds, or subconscious. It may not see the light of day, even though we know it's there. Everyone is capable of unjust, dark thoughts. Jesse Jackson once candidly admitted his culpability: "There is nothing more painful to me . . . than to walk down the street and hear footsteps and start thinking about robbery, then look around and see somebody white and feel relieved."[1]

Indeed, we must admit we are all fallible. I've been blessed to go on two mission trips to Rwanda. On my first, I visited the Kigali Genocide Museum with about 50 other members of the mission team. During the unsettling experience a young teen proudly declared he was so glad he would never fall prey himself to such flawed ideology. A wise onlooker simply told him we are all capable of it. Mother Jones said, "Injustice boils in men's hearts as does steel in its cauldron, ready to pour forth, white hot, in the fullness of time."[2]

First we must admit we're capable of prejudice, or worse, so we nip it in the bud. We must pray for discernment from the only true and righteous Judge about matters that are colored with potential prejudice. No matter how well-intentioned or rooted in the Word we are, we make snap judgments about others. We can't trust ourselves to treat them fairly in our flawed humanity. We need to truly ponder "what would Jesus do?"

The second component in combatting the seeds of injustice in our own hearts is to speak up when we see it occurring. Abstaining is not an option. Desmond Tutu once said if you're neutral in situations of injustice, you have chosen the side of the oppressor. "If an elephant has its foot on the tail of a mouse, and you say that you are neutral, the mouse will not appreciate your neutrality,"[3] he mused. When Satan plants seeds of discord, we need to tell him to get off our tail and get behind us.

⊶

Keys to Kingdom Living: Be accountable for seeds of injustice and pray for correction.

Doorpost: "You shall not distort justice, you shall not be partial, and you shall not take a bribe. For a bribe blinds the eyes of the wise, and perverts the words of the righteous."
Deuteronomy 16:19 (NASB)

INJUSTICE: MAKING AMENDS WITHIN MINISTRIES AND CHRISTIAN FRIENDSHIPS

*T*he rich dimension of the Christian friendship is unmatched in the secular world. No matter how close or celebrated or infamous a relationship may be, if Jesus is not at the center, no one involved will operate on as high a plane as a Christian friend does. As Christians, we follow the first and greatest commandment: love your neighbor as yourself. When we do that, we put the other person's needs on the same plane as ours—or even, in some cases, above our own.

When working together in ministries with people of like mind and purpose, it's easy to imagine that conflicts and injustices will not arise. Sometimes we might even be under the mistaken impression that we are best suited to ministries where this doesn't occur, so we believe that when conflict does arise, it's a sign that it's time to bail. But when we act on emotion and react from it without discernment or reason, we give in to what the Enemy wants: his trap to conquer and divide God's people.

God's Word tells us we are to be peacemakers, to love each other deeply, for "love covers over a multitude of sins" (1 Peter 4:8). When something is said in haste and not carefully worded, we must take precautions not to read too much into it. And if we recognize that we're guilty of this and it's pointed out to us, we must be ready and willing to apologize if we've offended.

It's important to take care of little skirmishes before they grow into a "Hatfield and McCoy" feud that may last for years

—28 years, in that infamous case. We must be continually ready and willing to forgive and be forgiven, for two very important reasons: we must do all we can to live at peace with everyone, as we read in Romans 12:18, and we must also work against any desire to instigate or propagate misunderstanding or discord. Extending armfuls of olive branches is more valuable than making our points in social media or in discussions or activities where disagreement arises.

The most important reason for adopting a peacekeeping lifestyle involves the give and take of forgiveness. Your life literally depends on it! We read in Matthew 6:15 that "if you refuse to forgive others their sins, your heavenly Father will not forgive your sins." According to Bible scholar Bruce M. Metzger,

> *"When we fail to forgive people . . . the devil has a stronghold on us. . . . We are implying that the sin of the offender is greater than the sins we committed against God. In other words, how can we repent and come to God, when we believe that the sins of others against us are greater than our sins against God? . . . We can't receive the righteousness of God through faith if we maintain and hold to our own self-righteousness before the eyes of God."* [1]

In light of that, being an instrument and proponent of peace is a win-win.

—⚷—

Keys to Kingdom Living: Embrace a peaceful lifestyle filled with grace among Christian friends.
Doorpost: "So then, if you bring your gift to the altar and . . . remember that your brother has something against you, leave your gift . . . and be reconciled to them; then come and offer your gift." Matthew 5:23-24 (NET)

INJUSTICE: TURNING OUR BACKS ON
PATHS OF REVENGE

*E*ver since Cain murdered his brother Abel out of anger and jealousy, revenge has played a part in earthly life. In Cain's warped mind, he believed God was treating Abel more favorably, even though Cain took shortcuts with his own required sacrifice to God while Abel didn't. In Abel's mind, he was getting revenge, but in fact Cain had done nothing to him at all.

Even in cases of true injustice, revenge can't ever right any wrong. One action can't undo another, and often the revengeful action ends up being more egregious than the original offense. The implication of the word "revenge" is to inflict hurt or harm on someone for something they committed, either against myself or someone else. If I gossip about you and you hear about it, you might be tempted to do the same. But often, revenge takes things up a notch. Like if someone cuts me off to snag a parking space I was waiting for, and I whip out a handgun and shoot the driver: stakes are wildly raised.

Whenever we're wronged, our indignation radar kicks into gear. Our sense of being unjustly dealt with rises up from a furious place, and we can think of nothing else than trying to right whatever wrong has occurred. But the biggest problem with homespun revenge is twofold: first of all, God is the only true and righteous Judge, and second of all, He promises to right every wrong and settle the score. So we need to bow out and let God be God, because we are not. "Vengeance is mine, I will repay . . ." says the Lord as recorded in Romans 12:19 (NKJV).

We're told in Proverbs 20:22, "Do not say, 'I will repay evil'; wait for the Lord, He will save you." We are actually warned in Leviticus 24:19 not to take revenge on another to avoid harm to ourselves. The passage reads, "If anyone injures his neighbor, as he has done it shall be done to him, fracture for fracture, eye for eye, tooth for tooth; whatever injury he has given a person shall be given to him" (ESV). This Scripture is frequently misinterpreted. People say "an eye for an eye" and quote the Bible to support the idea of enacting earthly, vigilante-style justice. But it really means is that if a person takes justice into their own hands, that person also deserves the same.

Jesus said He came not to abolish but to fulfill the law. We can trust that He will do that in every aspect of the law. Jesus also reminded us, "You have heard it was said to those of old, "You shall not murder; and whomever murders will be liable to judgment," to which Jesus replies, "But I say to you that everyone who is angry with his brother will be liable to judgment" (Matthew 5:22 ESV).

Finally, we are told to be reconciled to our brother, in Matthew 5:24. If a fellow Christian feels wronged by you, or vice versa, we are compelled to rectify the matter. And no matter what the issue, we are to leave justification to God.

⊢•⊷

Keys to Kingdom Living: Revenge is counter-intuitive to loving one another as Jesus did.
Doorpost: "Never take your own revenge, beloved, but leave room for the wrath of God, for it is written, 'Vengeance is mine, I will repay,' says the Lord." Romans 12:19 (NASB)

INJUSTICE: EVERY TEAR AND EVERY WRONG WIPED AWAY!

*J*n my younger (and more arrogant) days, my self-congratulatory muscle was in overdrive. My thinking was that my memory of past events was virtually infallible. I conceded that my short-term memory was plenty faulty, but when it came to so-called "times of my life," no detail escaped my total recall. Until one day my husband started talking about a concert we had attended some thirty years before. In that moment, I had absolutely no recollection of it whatsoever. As he recounted details to jog my memory, it came back to me. It was then I had to reconcile the fact that my delusions of total recall were inaccurate.

When it comes to our minds and the rest of our imperfect bodies, we are in fact completely fallible. Our judgment is as vulnerable as the rest of our mental faculties; in one moment we might exercise the fair thing, but in another we might be clouded from seeds of favoritism, retribution, or any number of subconscious prejudices that may color the pool of fairness. We are in no position to judge our own judgment.

In this instance, as in all others, we must look to Jesus. He alone is worthy to "open the scrolls" (see Revelation 4:11). The only non-corrupt mind is the mind of God Himself. So in any situation, we must follow His wise counsel. Instead of addressing someone's wrong move with one of your own, make the right move. Whether the issue is theft, loss, the unfair maligning of character, or something much more horrific like the taking of a life, we are still called to forgive and let God ultimately administer His perfect justice.

I have adopted a new coping strategy for times such as these. When someone hurts me or steals something from me, I remind myself of the verse in Joel 2:25 where God promises to repay us for the years the locusts "ate our crops." I visualize a pile of things, stolen from me throughout my lifetime, returned to me in more glorious condition—or I picture an image of a trying and unjust situation I've had to endure, and picture total restoration. It comforts me. I imagine my room in heaven filled with glorious family portraits that could never be taken because of my autistic child's inability to sit for such an undertaking. The thief of autism stole it—but God will restore it. He remains faithful to His promises. When I am wounded, I can trust the Great Healer to bind up my wounds. "Behold," He promises in Revelation 21:5, "I am making all things new" (ESV).

Next time you come face-to-face with an injustice, take your anger down a notch. Dim the lights; de-escalate the situation. Visualize God taking it by the reins while you sit back and benefit from His navigation.

—⚷—

Keys to Kingdom Living: Allow God to settle the score as He has promised He will.
Doorpost: "Trust in the Lord with all your heart and lean not on your own understanding." Proverbs 3:5

WEEK 5: FAILURE

FAILURE: IN KEEPING THE LAW

I heard a story about two high school students in contention for valedictorian. The tale spreading around school was that the race was neck-and-neck, with dueling GPAs, so the policy was to look back at previous grades. In the final analysis, a B earned in kindergarten cost one gal the title and, as a result, it went to the other contender.

It's enough to make this B student's head spin. A misstep incurred at five years old results in a reckoning at eighteen? The poor gal is sure to be inducted into the Slightly Unfair Moments Hall of Fame—but dem's the breaks, as the saying goes.

When it comes to keeping God's law, our report card doesn't even come close to the valedictorian contenders. Even if it did, coming close counts far more in horseshoes and hand grenades than it does in obeying the law. Only Jesus Christ kept the law perfectly, and anything less cannot qualify us for an eternity living with God except through the gate of the Good Shepherd. In our humanity we fail again and again, yet God continues to redeem, restore, and reinvigorate His people through the infinite power of His grace and the infusion of His Holy Spirit.

Because of this fail-safe plan God knew we'd need from the dawn of creation, we don't need to stay bogged down in failure. In our humanity, though, we might be tempted to relive our mistakes and even magnify them to an "unforgivable" status, but we are reminded over and over that our slates have already been wiped clean, and "with His stripes we are healed" (Isaiah 53:5 KJV).

We can rest in knowing that when we recommit to walking in God's will and truly delighting in His ways, we begin again on our journey to pursue holiness with passion and fervor, even if we can't master righteousness perfectly. When we repeatedly recommit to this process after a stumble, we remain faithful to a lifetime quest for obedience without letting the Enemy get a foothold in our insecurity.

God has given us many promises about this, but my favorite verse states that He "who began a good work in you will carry it on to completion until the day of Jesus Christ" (Philippians 1:6). In light of this uplifting guarantee, we are poised with God's help to overcome every failure of obedience to the law to triumph over the schemes of the Enemy. When we stay rooted in Him, He works through us to accomplish what would otherwise be completely impossible. What a friend we have in Jesus, the Perfecter of our faith!

—⚯—

Keys to Kingdom Living: God continually redeems and restores His repentant remnant.
Doorpost: "Though a righteous person falls seven times, he will get up, but the wicked will stumble into ruin." Proverbs 24:16 (CSB)

FAILURE: THE TRAP OF NON-FORGIVENESS

*I*n my travels to Rwanda, I've heard powerful testimonies about genocide victims forgiving the perpetrators of crimes against their families. I've heard incredible tales of restoration of the spirit and reconciliation among families in villages. These stories are far more powerful when they're told by the parties involved than they could ever be in my retelling. I witnessed a murderer come face-to-face with the survivors of one of his crimes. He testified to God's greatness in the healing in church and embraced them in one of the most powerful gestures of Christian love I have ever seen. The room was filled with the power of repentance and grace. When a comparatively minor grievance surfaces between me and someone else these days I may be tempted to hold a grudge, but this memory pops up and reminds me of the absurdity of anything less weighty. (Which is everything.)

Martin Luther King, Jr.'s infamous quote about forgiveness is even more poignant in the aftermath of his death than it was in his lifetime. If he had survived his assassination attempt, there is little doubt that he would have fully forgiven James Earl Ray —tried and convicted of the crime in 1969—based on these telling words: "We must develop and maintain the capacity to forgive. He who is devoid of the power to forgive is devoid of the power to love. There is some good in the worst of us and some evil in the best of us. When we discover this, we are less prone to hate our enemies."[1] Sadly, forty deaths resulted in the angry aftermath of that heinous crime, something that would no doubt have deeply grieved the man who said he wanted to be remembered as a man who tried to give his life serving.

More importantly, whether a grievance is minor or major, God requires forgiveness. He tells us in Matthew 6:15 that if we do not forgive others, we will not be forgiven by God. Offering forgiveness is a prerequisite to receiving it. When we fail to forgive, we fail to love, breaking the eleventh commandment of loving one another as Jesus Christ loved us. "They" are never going to know that we are Christians by our love if we don't have any to show. Worse yet, we ourselves will not be forgiven if we don't do the same for those who have wronged us, as we learn in Mark 11:25. Any break in relationship, whether in personal or societal, represents a break in communion not only with that group of people, but with God Himself. As Christians, we need to walk our talk and forgive the returning prodigal child as well as the terrorists we've never met. As tempting as it might be to shut the door on the prodigal coming back for forgiveness for the tenth time, or to harbor hatred for Muslims based on the terrorist actions of a fringe segment (that also warrants our forgiveness), these actions do not line up with what Jesus would do, were He walking the earth today. Will you stand with Him in doing the right thing, however hard or uncomfortable it might be?

⊶

Keys to Kingdom Living: Failure to forgive is the same as a failure to love as He loved us.
Doorpost: And whenever you stand praying, forgive, if you have anything against anyone, forgive him, so that your Father in heaven may also forgive your trespasses." Mark 11:25 (NKJV)

FAILURE: IN PARENTING

*A*ny mom or dad knows that when it comes to parenting, our moon-landing moments bear a sharp contrast to those times we spend sinking in quicksand. We reach a zenith of joy only to later find ourselves falling down an *Alice in Wonderland* hole of despair that feels like a bottomless pit as we wonder what we were thinking when we welcomed little people into our lives.

You might, like me, play a little tape in your head of historical snippets of situations in your child's life where you wish you'd done something differently. I remember once when something happened at school to my oldest son that he felt was unjust. As he told me about it, he said to me, "Mom, go down there and fix it!" I realized my son went into a rescue default when it came to some problem solving that he needed to do. I felt as if I'd failed to teach him self-advocating skills. From that point on, I vowed to step back and let him manage similar situations. Success varied in those endeavors (and still does today), but without that failure, I wouldn't have seen the need for the correction.

Though no one likes the feeling of failure, everyone is positioned to learn and grow from it. Parents in particular are uniquely positioned to devote themselves to growth and change as their children grow and change. Parents can hold fast to the truths that never change while adapting to appropriate levels of intervention as their children leave home to live their lives and raise their own offspring.

Our best parenting comes from a posture of being authentic with our kids. We need to share our own struggles, guide and direct them during theirs, and encourage and praise them when they do well rather than continually criticize. We need to pay special attention to not provoke them so they don't become discouraged, as we read in Colossians 3:21.

And when we do experience failure, it's good to remember Paul's wise counsel about what it means to carry on after a setback. In chapter 3 verse 13 of his letter to the Philippians, he reminds us that, when confronted with failure, we can put aside what is behind us and look forward to what lies ahead. We, too, can dust ourselves off and begin again to seek God's will as we parent our children from childhood to adulthood. As we do, we honor our heavenly Father. His example of discipline, forgiveness, and grace remains a timeless model we can adopt until the day we are all united with Him in the New Jerusalem.

᚛᚛᚛

Keys to Kingdom Living: Learn from failure in parenting, and move forward with confidence that God will provide insight to those who seek His ultimate wisdom.
Doorpost: "Whoever troubles his own household will inherit the wind, and the fool will be servant to the wise of heart." Proverbs 11:29 (ESV)

FAILURE: WITHIN SERVANT MINISTRY

*H*ow many of us have felt a call to a new ministry, put our heart and soul into getting it going, and then watched as it died a slow and painful death? Whether it's something small like a Christian meditation class, or something larger such as a church plant in an international capital city, not everything we touch on this earth is going to turn to gold, no matter how pure the motivation.

No matter how closely we feel we are tuned to what God is doing, sometimes a "red herring" will appear in the net with the other fish we've been bringing in for Jesus. By definition, a red herring refers to something distracting by nature that may be intentional or unintentional. Sometimes the Enemy will throw a red herring into a situation to create chaos and confusion where clarity once ruled, but sometimes one failed ministry births another of greater impact. One of our church pastors tells a story of bringing members together on a weekday to hear more in-depth teaching than what was offered on Sunday, intended to speak more to curious non-believers. This structure ambled along until it dawned on the pastor that meeting in smaller groups in homes would be a better use of the allotted time, so he mentioned it to his superior. The teaching night was discontinued, but it gave birth to a ministry that now has more members than the church counts as regular attendees.

As in many other areas of life, there are going to be times

where we simply don't understand what's going on with regards to God's plan. I remember an instance where I'd renewed a commitment to a certain ministry for a one-year increment. I was set to attend their annual retreat. Suddenly, before I left, I felt compelled to call a woman I had not seen in years about another ministry. I phoned her and she said she felt it was a sign that maybe I was supposed to work alongside her. These ministries met on the same day and I would have to choose. I prayed and was second-guessing my previous commitment. Conflicted, I discussed the situation with the other teaching director. She said they believed God did not call people out to work for another ministry after so much planning and prayer had gone into the process. Because I had committed to submitting to their authority, I remained. It was a blessed year of effective ministry where I'd originally pledged my time.

I never determined whether that other leading came from. Was it a red herring was designed by the devil to create chaos? It may have been a test of obedience or something else I've failed to understand this side of eternity. When we are moved in or out of ministries, we listen for God's leading as best we can, readying ourselves to bloom where planted or pack up and head to the next mission field.

─•✛

Keys to Kingdom Living: Readying ourselves for failure in ministry may pave the way for new challenges.
Doorpost: "Trust in the Lord with all your heart, and lean not on your own understanding." Proverbs 3:5

FAILURE: AN UNAVOIDABLE
BYPRODUCT OF PROACTIVITY

*A*s a young girl, I remember trying to avoid the sting of failure at all costs. I shied away from team pursuits as much as possible, not willing to trust others to accomplish their tasks in order to achieve joint success. I ran track, a solo sport, and preferred the solitary pleasures of snow skiing over team-based sports. I hated group projects at school. I became a reporter in part so I could be the only one primarily responsible for my work. I inherited this trait in part from my mother: she would always shoo me away when I tried to help her with something, flatly stating (albeit ungrammatically) that "nobody does on my deals."

I even went so far as to not attempt a certain thing because all odds appeared against it. But this runs counter to what God wants for us, as we learn in the parable of the talents found in Matthew 25. In the parable, a man entrusts various sums of money to three of his servants. Two out of the three took what was given them and delivered an increase based on their efforts. But the third dug a hole and hid the sum underground, much to the distress of his supervisor.

When we sequester our money or squander our talents by not listening to God's call, we're not honoring God. Each of us has a unique set of gifts and our own earthly resources to work with in this life. An arsenal of monetary and spiritual gifts that never see the light of day can't further God's kingdom. In some respects, we can even hinder it when we don't do our part. We know "the earth is the Lord's and everything in it," based on what is written in 1 Corinthians 10:26. So if we fail at a task using our time or talents, we are still actively using what God has given us. When He calls us to generosity, regarding our time, spiritual gifts, and tithing, He expects proactivity as opposed to inactivity.

As I got older, I realized in many ways I was guilty of this inactivity. *Why give small amounts of money to ministries? It won't make a real difference,* I thought. Or I would tell myself one extra pair of hands wouldn't be missed in a sea of volunteers. But when God calls us to anything, only He knows His plans and purposes in it. We're in no place to judge what does or doesn't make a difference.

Today I push my inactivity envelope. I've got three more books planned. I'm involved in a global outreach mission team that's been life-changing for hundreds of people. Since launching "Operation Proactivity" in my life, I've seen that I need God's help on all of my "deals." After all, He's the God of the impossible, as we learn in Luke 1:37. Though God doesn't guarantee us success in everything we touch, we're told of His love for the cheerful giver in 2 Corinthians 9:7. Being a real blessing to God is a truly rich reward that we can realize when we serve in all the ways God wired us to give.

Keys to Kingdom Living: Choosing to invest time and talents for the Lord pays eternal dividends.
Doorpost: "As each has received a gift, use it to serve one another, as good stewards of God's varied grace." 1 Peter 4:10 (ESV)

FAILURE: AS A PRECURSOR FOR
REBIRTH AND RENEWAL

he authors of *To Kill a Mockingbird*, *Moby Dick*, and *Gone with the Wind* all have one thing in common: their books were initially rejected by publishers. Thomas Edison was fired from his first two jobs and made over 1,000 attempts at creating the light bulb before he struck invention gold. Abraham Lincoln lost six elections of various types before being elected as one of the greatest presidents America has ever known. Surely all of these men and women were tempted to give up after experiencing multiple defeats. But because they didn't, their names are preserved in the annals of history.

Much is made of successful people after they've achieved their goals, but much can be learned from failure. A well-known historical quote says, "Our greatest glory is not in never failing but in rising every time we fail."[1] This truth is an important hallmark of the Christian faith. We cannot remain prostrate if we fall down. Proverbs 14:32 states, "The wicked are crushed by disaster, but the godly have a refuge" (NLT). Because we are assured of our eternal inheritance, we can put earthly failure in perspective. We know we will reap a harvest in due time, even if we must suffer through years of disappointment and occasionally even catastrophe.

This is easier said than done. Fortunately we have a wealth of examples from which to learn. Many an individual in the Bible rose like a proverbial phoenix from their ashes of disgrace.

David is probably one of the most famous. After he seduced Bathsheba and had her husband Uriah killed, he had to come to terms with his moral failing. He repented, and although there were consequences to his sin, we now enjoy the fruit of what came out of his failure whenever we read Psalms. God helps us dust ourselves off to persevere in that same way. His commitment to plans and purposes for our lives never wavers, even if we can't always feel or internalize it. In Isaiah 41:9 we read, "I brought you from the ends of the earth, I called you from its farthest corners. I said, 'You are my servant.' I have chosen and not rejected you" (BSB).

If you have sought God's voice in committing to your plans and purposes, making sure they are in alignment with His, He will bring you the success He sees fit for your life, in His timing, and in His fashion. These dreams might not feel as if they are always in alignment with your own. However, it's important to stay connected to Him in prayer, seeking His direction. We must diligently guard against being dragged down by the quagmire of negative feelings connected with failure. We can view failures as a learning process rather than a slam of the brakes. God walked with David through his post-failure restoration, and He will walk us through ours as well. He will never leave us or forsake us.

⸻⊖

Keys to Kingdom Living: Failure is a stepping stone God can use to build our faith, help us learn from our mistakes, and teach us to persevere to achieve His goals for us.
Doorpost: "If God is for us, who can be against us?" Romans 8:31

FAILURE: A CATALYST FOR TOTAL RELIANCE ON GOD

One of the fondest memories I have about my trip to Florence is seeing Michelangelo's statue of David in the Galleria dell'Accademia. A large circular room with a beautiful domed ceiling is devoted to showcasing its majesty. In listening to the commentary regarding the artist's approach to the work, I learned that Michelangelo deliberately positioned David's sling behind him. It was the artist's intention to minimize the weapon young David used in order to magnify God's power as the primary component in his victory. If you walk around to the back of the statue, you can see how the fabric of the sling clings seamlessly to David's back, almost disappearing into the sculpture. Indeed, the beauty of the story of David is how God took a young man with an inferior weapon to bring about His victory against a seemingly undefeatable giant.

In life as in art, God is worthy of the honor and glory in every success we achieve. But in our pride, we sometimes fail to acknowledge His part in them, so occasionally God will use little failures to bring about refinement in us. In Judges 7, we read of the story of Gideon. We're told in verse 2 that God deliberately reduced the size of Gideon's army from a starting number of 22,000 men down to 300 to cut off any future pride at the pass. "The Israelites will boast to me that they saved themselves by their own strength" (NLT).

God, of course, knows that we haven't the strength to save

ourselves; we are the ones He must continually remind. David himself aptly wrote that God's Word is a lamp unto our feet and a light to our path in Psalm 119:105. God doesn't give us a map of our life from beginning to end and a floodlight so we can see into our future until the day we die. Instead, He desires a day-to-day relationship. He assists us in our struggles and failures and spurs us on with His Holy Spirit to provide the hope we need to face our future with confidence that He alone is in control, when we commit to Him.

Those who don't know Jesus cannot experience this vital confidence. They are to a great degree alone in their struggles without the benefit of consulting their Wonderful Counselor. But even those of us who belong to Him often fail to take advantage of the indispensable benefit of God's wisdom in our war rooms. It's always available to us, either in the form of quiet time or via the advice and encouragement of His servants on earth. Not using this important tool is like squandering a gift certificate. We need to fully rely on God and honor His role in our victories. We must look at both failure and success from an eternal perspective. God knows His plans for our future as long as we are following His road map.

ᴏᴡᴏ

Keys to Kingdom Living: God sometimes allows failure before He orchestrates victory so we rely more fully on Him.
Doorpost: "He gives power to the faint, and to him who has no might he increases strength." Isaiah 40:29 (ESV)

WEEK 6: COMBATTING LONELINESS

COMBATTING LONELINESS:
PERSONAL ISOLATION

Picture it: the requisite breakup scene in a movie where the "dumpee" is sprawled out on the couch. She's rumpled, with tangled hair and smeared mascara, donning baggy sweatpants. A sappy movie is on her television. Pints of Ben & Jerry's—empty and full—are lined up the coffee table rim. But by movie's end, we watch as her problems are obscured with a bright red bow because someone else has appeared to share the ice cream with. If only life's isolation was this easily solved!

Often, when we're hurting, we want to use Greta Garbo's most famous movie line from the movie *Grand Hotel*: we "vant to be alone." Our tendency to withdraw in our misery seems natural in a "don't worry, be happy" world. We may choose to withdraw even as caring friends try to come alongside to help share our burden. You may have been on both sides of this equation. You may have been the caring friend whose phone calls and attempts to reach out to a friend in isolation and pain have gone unanswered. Or you may have been the grief-stricken individual who was holed up and feeling so raw you couldn't muster enough energy or gumption to let anyone else in, no matter how loving their attempts to reach out might have been.

The truth is, when we are in these situations, we are battling more than just our own grief and pain. We are battling an Enemy who loves nothing more than to take us down to the depths of despair. He's doing his best to make sure that the message of hope never reaches the ears that so desperately need to hear it. In The Message translation we read in Galatians 6:2, "Stoop down and reach out to those who are oppressed. Share their burdens, and so complete Christ's law. If you think you are too good for that, you are badly deceived." We are much less likely to be deceived or to stay in the pit when others are coming alongside. In Ecclesiastes 4:12, we read, "Though one may be overpowered, two can defend themselves. A cord of three strands is not easily broken."

I know my cord sometimes feels like it's about to unravel. Shortly after I found out my youngest son had autism, friends came over and sat with me in my pajamas when I felt like I couldn't move a single fiber of my being except for my tear ducts. They didn't pass judgment or lecture. They just came over to love me and gently remind me of God's promises.

I'm blessed with genuine friends who deeply care about me and are willing to come alongside to help me bear my most heartbreaking burdens. Aside from their genuine concern for my welfare, they take their role as a follower of Christ and the responsibilities that come along with it very seriously. Knowing and truly understanding this part of Scripture helps us to combat the spiritual warfare that comes our way by both giving and accepting caring intervention.

Keys to Kingdom Living: Reject seclusion. Accept and offer comfort in times of trial.

Doorpost: "One who isolates himself pursues selfish desires; he rebels against all sound wisdom." Proverbs 18:1 (CSB)

COMBATTING LONELINESS: ALLEVIATING LONELINESS IN YOUR FAMILY

There are times in my home when my husband is watching sports, my oldest is gaming on his iPad, my youngest is looking at pictures, and I'm glued to the television, binge-watching Hallmark movies. I imagine someday I will look back on this and regret not having insisted on playing more board games or interacting as a unit of four as opposed to four parties of one. I'm not advocating for mandated 24/7 group activities. But I do think in an era in which personal entertainment vies for our attention, we need to make an effort to structure some group activity to counteract it.

Two kinds of loneliness are particularly concerning in the technological age: social and emotional. Social loneliness refers to the aloneness felt when we self-isolate or are left out of certain groups. Emotional loneliness is the second type; it may be experienced within the family unit when someone is not getting his or her emotional needs fully met. This could include a spouse who is ignored or marginalized by their partner or a teenager who feels misunderstood by his parents. It can also include the elderly parent. They might live in a household with an adult child but perhaps aren't included in all family activities —for a variety of reasons—and feel marginalized as a result.

God knew from the moment He created Adam from the dust of the earth that something was missing. In Genesis 2 we read how God formed that family unit of Adam and Eve. Soon after, sin crouched at the door, and the family has struggled ever since. But today Satan doesn't take on the familiar snake form. He prefers a more stealth presence in the twenty-first century. He's front and center in violent video games, desensitizing our youth to the taking of human life. Evil might rear its ugly head with the spreading of lies, rumors, or bullying in a group text. Satan delights in the proliferation of online pornography accessible with the click of a button to an isolated spouse or a curious ten-year-old boy.

The best way to combat these influences is to be mindful of each family member. Make sure you invest wisely and lavishly with regard to the amount and quality of the time you and your family members spend with one another. Build the family dinner into your week. Mandate a no-device rule at the dinner table. If you are able, designate a day for the family to spend together in a social activity. It may be a community picnic, dinner out at a restaurant, or an activity such as bowling or miniature golf that builds memories and offers an opportunity for meaningful conversation. When we invest in our families, we bring honor and glory to God. But when we contribute to their demise through selfishness or neglect, we bring destruction. We read in Proverbs 11:29 that "whoever troubles his own household will inherit the wind, and the fool will be servant to the wise of heart" (BSB).

—⦿—

Keys to Kingdom Living: Invest genuine love and time to combat whatever threatens to conquer and divide your precious family unit.

Doorpost: "It is not good for the man to be alone." Genesis 2:18

COMBATTING LONELINESS: INCLUSIVE SOLUTIONS FOR OSTRACIZED COMMUNITY GROUPS

*S*ome of society's biggest problems seem too daunting to undertake. How do you properly and effectively address the loneliness of a prison inmate with a reasonable dose of compassion, yet still protect society? What does social inclusion look like for a homeless person, or for the drug abuser on the streets? These are tough questions with no simple answers or cut-and-dried solutions.

Many of you reading this struggle with the fact that someone you love fits into one of these categories of marginalized society. While a general attitude of hands-off care exists for these groups, when it comes to people actually willing to roll up their sleeves and get their hands dirty, fewer individuals step up to the plate. Probably one of the best examples on how to alleviate the loneliness of this struggling segment of the population is to look at the Good Samaritan and what he did and didn't do in Luke 10. What he didn't do: pass by the trouble without reacting. He didn't let the long-standing prejudice of the victim's nationality impair his judgment call to help him. He didn't bring him home with him and take him in to live with him for the rest of their lives. What he did do was rescue him from the road, treat and bind up his wounds, take him to an inn, and paid the innkeeper for days in the room while he recuperated.

Sometimes we look at problems that seem too large to solve and think it's better to walk away completely rather than to intervene if we can't completely eradicate them. But Jesus Himself said in Matthew 26:11 that we will always have the poor. This side of eternity, poverty can never be fully eliminated. But that doesn't mean we are free to walk away and wash our hands of any responsibility to our fellow human beings in need.

The church life group we attend builds in seasonal visits to feed the homeless in a shelter. We provide a hot meal for evening and a lunch for the next day. We help sort and distribute used clothing donations. We look them straight in the eye and treat them with the dignity and respect that any child of God deserves whether they belong to Him or not. We don't lecture or pretend that we can solve their long-term problems or invite them to come home and live with us. But we do what we can in a safe, organized, and caring environment to love them like Jesus would.

Some may read this and wonder what good something like that really does. In my humanity, I understand their viewpoint and might even share it if it weren't for what God's Word says on the matter. I look at Matthew 25:35-40 and recall Jesus's words about nourishing, housing, and clothing the needy: "Whatever you did for one of the least of these brothers and sisters of mine, you did for me." It may be a drop in the overall bucket and not inclined to erase the problems in the world, yet I'll add my humble drops knowing He is pleased and glorified.

⊢••••⊖

Keys to Kingdom Living: God's people deserve to be loved, cared for, and included.
Doorpost: "Truly I tell you, whatever you did for one of the least of these brothers and sisters of mine, you did for me." Matthew 25:40

COMBATTING LONELINESS: REACHING OUT TO WIDOWS AND ORPHANS

*B*efore embarking on Rwanda mission trips, I was clueless about the harsh realities and pervasiveness of the desperate widows and orphans. During the 100 days of the Rwandan genocide and the systematic killing of 800,000 to 1 million citizens, 50,000 widows were left behind to care for their families. Approximately 75,000 orphans were left to care for themselves without any surviving parent or extended family member available to take them in. Though orphanages have tried to accommodate this staggering remnant, over 40,000 orphans still fend for themselves without the protection of a shelter of any kind.

As I write this, years after my visit, the faces that make up these statistics haunt me. The widows forge ahead, some trying their best to care for their family by growing crops and working in the coffee and tea fields with their babies on their backs. Others too old to work rely on what the church can do to help them get by. Some orphans have been taken in by local families and have their secondary education sponsored by American citizens who've seen the need to help these young people emerge from their cycle of poverty.

God's Word is very clear about the responsibility Christians have to care for these very vulnerable segments of the population. James writes in his letter, in chapter one, verse seven, that this care is a religion that "God our Father accepts as pure and faultless." He speaks in particular here to pompous individuals who consider themselves "religious" but who are more inclined to pontificate about their good works than to roll up their sleeves and actually do them.

I will never forget my experience in Rwanda when a woman who was widowed came up to me after I had spoken to the congregation about the loaves and fishes principle of how God multiplied little into much. "I am hungry," she said, looking me straight in the eye. Unlike her, I knew I had the ability and means to get food later, back at our modest motel. So I reached into my backpack and grabbed a handful of trail mix. No, it didn't solve her hunger problem long-term. But what kind of Christian would I be if I didn't respond in love and do *something* to help her out? We need to walk our talk.

Closer to home, this care looks a little different. I try to reach out to women I know who have been widowed. One woman in particular has no children and few living relatives, so I invite her for breakfast or lunch or just stop by to make sure she's ok from time to time. It's my hope and prayer that if I'm ever on the other end of that scenario that someone would care enough to reach out to me as well with friendship, love, and an occasional side order of bacon.

—⊕—

Keys to Kingdom Living:
Do your part, however small it may seem, to walk your talk with those in need.
Doorpost: "Look after orphans and widows in their distress and . . . keep oneself from being polluted in the world." James 1:27

COMBATTING LONELINESS:
EMBRACING SINGLES AT CHURCH

*W*hen I was younger, I remember my parents had a kind of unspoken arrangement that if one was not going to make it to church, the other stayed home too. The implication was that sitting in church alone did not feel good to them or was somehow perceived as unacceptable, either by one or the other. As I grew older, I realized that they weren't alone with this line of thinking. There are people who won't eat in a restaurant or go to the movies alone either. But I also saw that plenty of people—either by choice or because of their family demographic—were perfectly willing to sit in the pew by themselves.

Fortunately when I was a single person I didn't have a problem with going to church by myself. Traveling alone on business in my younger days conditioned me to solitary pursuits. As a single, consistency was more of a problem than lack of company. In college, I actually enjoyed showing up at sacred spaces in the evening, in between services, for private prayer and reflection. When I married and we adopted our sons, the notion of being surrounded by family took on a different significance. It was less about Christian community and more about parading my babies in their dapper duds as we sauntered off to a nice lunch.

Of course, that was early on. New lessons awaited me when my oldest began playing in the student ministry band. Suddenly,

I had to drive him to early practices and my husband was taking our special needs son to a different campus in our church that was miles away from where the four of us lived. Because my oldest had to play two services, I began sitting by myself. At first I felt irritated but then began to join another couple in worship who have since become dear friends. This experience prompted me to become more aware of those sitting alone, just as it has raised the awareness level of my being alone for others around me.

Unlike many others who sit alone in church, I don't live alone or struggle with too much alone time. Both individuals and churches need to reach out to these singles who may be a family of one or worshipping alone for extenuating circumstances. Too often the emphasis on singles ministry involves trying to connect singles to encourage marriage. Sadly, this leaves out the married man or woman whose spouse stays home or the elderly widow or widower who may not seek another mate in their remaining years on earth. Coming alongside doesn't have to involve a long-term agenda. Sharing coffee before a service or welcoming a single to sit with you is a little kindness that might mean more to them than you know.

⊢——β

Keys to Kingdom Living: Reach out to those around you who go through life alone in big and small ways.
Doorpost: "Two are better than one, because they have a good reward for their labor . . . But woe to anyone who falls and has no one to help them up." Ecclesiastes 4:9-10

COMBATTING LONELINESS: COMING ALONGSIDE THE SICK

*T*here are three kinds of patients: those who want, and maybe even need, constant attention and assistance; patients who would prefer to hibernate in a cave; and those who fall somewhere between this divergent spectrum.

I'm probably a middle ground girl. Hibernation is great for sleep, but I love it when a card arrives when I'm recovering from something that has kept me out of the social loop for a couple of weeks. Everyone appreciates gestures of concern and care on some level—even hibernators. And anyone who's ever been sick for any length of time, especially those with contagion concerns or those who suffer illness with social stigmas, isolation can be a huge problem. Ask someone who had the Ebola virus. It is for these folks that terms like "don't touch them with a ten-foot pole" were invented.

Jesus did a perfect job of modeling ministry to the marginalized sick. He touched the untouchable: lepers and women who were bleeding, both considered "unclean" by Jewish statutes. Jesus always put people over conventions and considered love the highest calling. He always acknowledged their dignity. He asked many if they wanted to be healed. In John 5:6 we read that Jesus saw a paralyzed man lying down and when He learned that the man had endured his condition for a long time, Jesus said to him, point blank, "Do you want to be healed?" This is a point in the story that is sometimes missed. Not everyone takes steps to facilitate healing or even really wants it. A handful of individuals remain resigned to sickness and all that is connected with it, for a variety of reasons.

What keeps us from reaching out to the sick? Are we afraid of contagion? Reasonable steps can be taken. Are we worried that care of the sick will suck the life out of our schedule? I remember a friend who was diagnosed with cancer during one of the busiest seasons in my life. God made Himself very clear that she was to take priority and I was to lay down my schedule and make it to every chemo appointment possible, to the very best of my ability. Though my to-do list was impacted, my compassionate heart grew, and my priorities underwent a dramatic shift. Other people's deep needs trump errands and the like. Jesus always put people first, and we can, too. Even small actions like bringing a meal, providing a grocery store gift card, or driving someone to a doctor's appointment are significant to someone who is suffering.

⊶

Keys to Kingdom Living: Listen to God's leadings on how you can help the sick, whether they are family members, close friends, or a marginalized segment of society.

Doorpost: "How can one keep warm alone? And though a man might prevail against one who is alone, two will withstand him—a threefold cord is not quickly broken." Ecclesiastes 4:11-12 (ESV)

COMBATTING LONELINESS: ELEANOR RIGBY AND BEYOND

"*A*ll the lonely people/Where do they all come from/All the lonely people/Where do they all belong?"[1]

These famous lines, written in large part by Paul McCartney and John Lennon, come from a song entitled "Eleanor Rigby," which explores the life of a lonely person, and others like her, who live life below society's feel-good radar. It's easy to miss this segment of society as we move through the routine machination of our lives, but the truth is Eleanor Rigbys are all around us. They are in behind us in line as we order from the barista. They are in the mall at the table across from you, eating their lunch in silence. They are alone in their house, staring at the dull glow of their television as you drive home from a Christmas party.

I remember the first time I heard "Eleanor Rigby." The song struck a raw nerve. I was a teen exploring these and other profound lyrics of a generation of malcontents. I was not alone. That song touched people around the world, with people everywhere who knew the pain of moments of loneliness as well as those who endured utter solitude. Here in America, single person households are more common than ever. Some of these people work, get out, and socialize, while others remain isolated except for occasional errands outside the home.

Caring, compassionate Christians, and their church groups need to reach out to this growing segment of the population. They need to find meaningful, creative ways beyond the typical young singles social events and delivery ministries for shut-ins. By comparison, individuals who live alone, between the ages of thirty-five and seventy-five, remain almost entirely untargeted by mainstream churches. Internet groups like Meetup.com are linking people together, but the linking of individuals for friendship and recreation lags behind.

We help turn the tide of loneliness when we reach out individually. I've been praying for the Lord to increase not only my awareness but my empathy to the "Eleanors" in my social sphere. An even more difficult but necessary prayer: opening my schedule. Invite someone you think might be fairly isolated to your house for lunch or to meet for coffee. You might be surprised what a blessing it can be, not only to them but also to you.

Jesus tried to unpack what true Christian love is all about in Matthew 25:35. He stands with those who responded in love to God's people saying, "I was a stranger and you invited me in." Then in verse 37, the righteous listeners ask the Lord, "When did we see you a stranger and invite you in?" In verse 40, Jesus replies, "Whatever you did for one of the least of these brothers and sisters of mine, you did for me."

—⦶⦿

Keys to Kingdom Living: Befriending the lonely has temporal and eternal benefits.
Doorpost: "But pity anyone who falls and has no one to help them up." Ecclesiastes 4:10

WEEK 7: DODGING SELF-ESTEEM BARBS

DODGING SELF-ESTEEM BARBS: THE UNWORTHINESS TRAP

*H*ow we view ourselves involves a delicate dance. We should strive to be self-actualized, meaning we should aim to achieve our full potential through creativity, independence, spontaneity, and a grasp of the real world as it pertains to our place in it. Keeping our own view in check is like trying to fill a balloon with enough helium to help it rise but taking care not to overfill so as to cause it to pop.

Paul talks about self-estimation in Romans 12:3, where he warns them not to think more of themselves than they ought, but also encourages them to think of themselves with sober judgment. Just as sober judgment protects against a too-high opinion of ourselves, it also guards against an unrealistic sense of unworthiness that may plague us from time to time. Overinflated perceptions are easier to spot than underinflated estimations in others and even in ourselves at times, but they are equally detrimental to our spiritual growth and effectiveness as kingdom workers.

The Enemy loves to fuel the fire of feelings of unworthiness. He does this by reminding us of the worst of our sins, which is a trap in itself since 1) God views all sins equally, and 2) we are all new creations in Christ, perpetually redeemed and sanctified when we confess wrongdoing and accept His gracious forgiveness. Another way Satan tries to undermine our self-esteem is by reminding us via negative talk about how inferior we are. I know plenty of people who feel too unworthy even to come to the Lord in prayer. They ask others to pray for them, not because they want more prayer warriors on their cause but because they think individuals more righteous than they are will have a better chance at gaining the favorable answer they seek.

Feelings of unworthiness needlessly distance us from a God who sacrificed the Son to build the life-giving bridge that links us to Him through His unfathomable grace. These negative feelings also tend to stagnate us from moving on to the next step in leadership or even participatory roles in ministries. Fortunately, God's Word offers a cornucopia of verses to help us fill our cups when they feel drip-dry to us. We are "the apple of [God's] eye," as recorded in Zechariah 2:8. In Luke 12:7 we read that even the hairs on our heads are numbered. God took great care to fashion us, and He oversees our lives, according to His will, with His plans and purposes in mind.

Striving to maintain an unbiased view of our talents, motives, and abilities, balanced with a healthy realization of where they all come from and should remain rooted, helps us situate ourselves to be of optimum use to God. I've had great success taping such promises onto a medicine cabinet to view them daily. Journaling verses about God's love can also remind us of our true worth in His eyes.

＊＊＊

Keys to Kingdom Living: Fill your balloon with the precious pearls of God's Word, verses that remind you of His love for you, so you will defy gravity and soar.

Doorpost: "Therefore, do not throw away your confidence, which has a great reward." Hebrews 10:35 (NASB)

DODGING SELF-ESTEEM BARBS: THE APPEARANCE TRAP

You ou may have heard the expression "if looks could kill . . ." But these days, lack of superlative good looks are killing the self-esteem of men and women alike as they try to compete with airbrushed celebrity images.

We can read 1 Samuel 16:7—"Man looks on the outward appearance, but the Lord looks on the heart" (ESV)—until we are blue in the face, but to deeply discern this truth is another matter entirely. You don't need a tutorial on the overemphasis of looks in today's culture. In an era of plastic surgery, hair extensions, lash enhancement, Spanx, personal fashion consultants, and retouched photos, leaving the house without hours of preparation would be unthinkable for a celebrity. The average young girl, who played with fashion model dolls for most of her life and has grown up viewing an avalanche of doctored photos in magazines or online, often feels hopelessly inadequate when looking at her own real body and face.

To the non-divine eye, David was not king material. He was not tall or particularly handsome. Samuel was presented a parade of candidates fitting the calendar-boy criteria—but God, much to Samuel's surprise, chose David. God knew the appearance of David's heart, and it was all that mattered to Him. God is actually counter-cultural when it comes to appearance. We read in 1 Peter 3:3-4 that we are not to only aim for external beauty with regard to elaborate hair, jewelry, or clothing. Peter goes on to say that, ideally, our adorning should be "the hidden person of the heart with the imperishable beauty of a gentle and quiet spirit, which in God's sight is very precious."

In whose sight should we most want to appear precious? The answer isn't our boyfriend, our spouse, dating site "trollers," or construction workers. The answer is God. His is the only opinion that matters. Sadly, even in Christian circles, appearance sometimes figures into positions of leadership in unfortunate, non-Biblical ways. In one women's Bible study, ladies considered overweight by other leaders might be passed over or removed from leadership, even though God's Word states He looks at the heart (and not the scale!). Another woman I know tells of being teased in Sunday school as a young girl about her clothing, which didn't flaunt the popular designer labels of the time. This memory scarred her and kept her away from church for years.

We mustn't allow popular culture—or even misguided Christians—to devalue us based on appearance opinions. We're made in God's image. Anyone finding fault with that needs to take a closer look at God's Word and His definition of beauty, which emanates from the inside out, instead of vice versa. When we view our bodies as instruments rather than ornaments, we reflect a healthy, God-pleasing attitude about who we are . . . and *whose* we are.

⊶⊸

Keys to Kingdom Living: Look at yourself through God's eyes from the outside in.
Doorpost: "For we are God's handiwork, created in Christ Jesus . . ." Ephesians 2:10

DODGING SELF-ESTEEM BARBS: THE PERFECT PERFORMANCE TRAP

*W*henever I see a wrinkled item of clothing, a sense of dread casts an imposing shadow over me. My fear of not being able to iron something perfectly stops me from even trying. I can still hear the consternation of my mother, who was a perfectionist in her undertakings. She would see something I'd attempted to iron and find great fault with it. Thankfully, I am living in the age of permanent press and dry cleaning.

Most of us experience a performance trap like this that prevents us from undertaking or completing tasks because we're pretty sure we can't satisfy our inner critic. This inner critic stems from lies the Enemy loves to tell you about yourself. He wants you to wallow in your imperfections so you will be rendered paralyzed and afraid to undertake the tasks God has set before you. Ironically God, the Author and Perfecter of our faith (Hebrews 12:2), not only knows we aren't perfect, He graciously accepts our imperfections. His "power is made perfect in weakness" (2 Corinthians 12:9).

The quest for perfectionism only serves to enslave the victim and serve the master of the inner critic who is never satisfied. In fact, when we strive for perfectionism we are placing more importance on a task than God is by trying to appease something inside of you, which doesn't reflect a godly motive. Any extra time needlessly spent on perfecting something might even detract from service God wants you to undertake but which you find you have no leftover time to accomplish.

Sometimes the stronghold of perfectionism is so fierce that it discourages people from trying to follow Christ at all. Like the wrinkled clothing that prompts dread in me, the idea of trying to lead a clean and righteous life feels too impossible to try to undertake. Fortunately, the God of grace and mercy that we serve recognizes that we sin and "fall short" (Romans 3:23). When men were ready to stone the woman caught in adultery in John 8:10-11, Jesus told the crowd that whoever was without sin was welcome to pick up the first stone. No one present was able to do that, but Jesus, who was without sin, instead told her that even He did not condemn her, but that she should go and sin no more.

While it's true we will never be able to say we lead perfect lives this side of eternity, we can follow the Perfect One to the best of our ability, confessing failures without wallowing in them, pressing on with confidence, thanks to His perfect grace.

⊢••⊕

Keys to Kingdom Living: Do things well for the Lord while taking care not to give into the trap of perfectionism.

Doorpost: "Martha, Martha, you are worried and bothered and anxious about many things; but only one thing is necessary, for Mary has chosen the good part . . . which shall not be taken away from her." Luke 10:41-42 (AMP)

DODGING SELF-ESTEEM BARBS: THE FAILURE TRAP

*I*n the movie *The Hunger Games*, Katniss Everdeen and her young sidekick Rue eye a cache of supplies in a middle of an open field. It's designed to entice as well as entrap the duo into an ambush, a notion they are painfully aware of. A profound quote by author and motivational speaker Jack Canfield sums up this and other similar scenarios: "Everything you want is on the other side of fear."[1]

Many of my good friends are fearless in the face of challenges. My admiration of this quality in them, as well as my shame that I don't possess it, is probably what draws me to them all the more. Fear of failure or ridicule has kept me from attempting many things I might have tried to accomplish—things like pie-in-the-sky jobs, dramatic weight loss, grueling exercise regimens, and other lofty ambitions.

In my frail humanity, I'm simply not willing to risk losing face if the odds are stacked too greatly against me. I'm pretty sure I'm not alone. In fact, in *The Hunger Games*, pawns of the government are always placating the endangered with a "may the odds be ever in your favor" tagline. The irony in the movie is that no one played by the rules. In fact, the gamekeeper's modus operandi was to manipulate things with ever more perilous directions—and some characters, hopelessly defeated, simply gave up.

Life can feel like the odds are never in our favor. But when we look to God to help us discern levels of palatable risk, we can accomplish things He has in mind for us to do. A friend's young daughter, gifted in fine art as well as dramatics, had her heart set on getting a role in the high school play. She poured all her energies into trying to land it, only to find her hopes dashed when she was passed over. A few days later, she found out that a piece of artwork she created was selected from dozens of other entries for the cover of the school's Christmas program playbill. Later that year, she put herself out there again by trying out for honors choir and was accepted. Best of all, she was selected to help assimilate incoming freshman into her school's mentoring program. Had God not grown her through setbacks, and had she not kept setting her fears aside, she would not have achieved all God intended for her own life as well as for those she is now destined to touch.

We never know which situations will result in our chance to shine or which will be chalked up to a failed attempt. But we should "press on," as Paul says in Philippians 3:14. Of all the authors of the Bible, no one had to fight more than Paul to overcome past failures. He was a terrorist-turned-lifesaver for God's eternal kingdom. His uphill battle of converting Christian souls in hostile environments would have been enough to cause many less dedicated and tenacious souls to hang up their proverbial hats. What opportunity are you running away from that God wants you to try to seize?

———⚷

Keys to Kingdom Living: Fight your inclination to give up on goals and dreams to break through the ceiling of complacency with God's help.

Doorpost: "In their hearts, humans plan their course, but the Lord establishes their steps." Proverbs 16:9

DODGING SELF-ESTEEM BARBS: THE TRAP OF CIRCUMSTANCE

To some degree, we're all like a vinyl record album. We have our hit side, the one the public sees, and our lesser-known flip side. Our friends, acquaintances, and even people like the mailman are all familiar with your hit side. It's the one with the upbeat, catchy tune. The hit side chronicles our successes, joys, triumphs, and our very best photos on social media, in conversations, and in the white space on our on annual Christmas cards. But when it comes to our flip side, it usually plays second fiddle.

Fewer people are privy to your flip side unless you make it a point to turn over your record. My flip side might include a suburban fashion editor job I didn't get back in the '80s, my struggles with infertility, the ravages of autism on my patience, and the stress and resentment the associated behaviors can induce when allowed to run amok. But like a rock that can be turned over to reveal a colony of living things, your flip side can also offer others a glimpse of a transformation in you that can't be ascertained from the hit side. In my own life, I would even go so far as to say that without the flip side, an authentic hit side distinguished by genuine joy would not be possible.

Sometimes our hit side blames our flip side for setbacks, and we shelve our record so neither side is played. Our perception is that the problems we endure, the battles we wage daily, and the cards we were dealt enslave us to such a degree that we take ourselves out of circulation altogether. I remember during the early years of dealing with the fallout of autism in my toddler, my inclination was to cut off all social contact. Even when I tried to connect with other moms who were going through similar circumstances, mine felt so much worse that I convinced myself no one truly understood. This further isolated me to the point where I had no one left to turn to who could help me climb out of the hole I'd dug for myself.

All this changed for me when I finally met someone who perfectly modeled handling her circumstances with inimitable grace. I sat on a park bench with her and shared my burden with her. She took time to carefully listen to me, and I knew she was truly sharing my burden in that moment. During our conversation, I learned that she had lost a child who had been very ill for most of his young life. When I asked her how she could possibly bear such a crushing blow, she smiled and said that God and His people in their love and grace help her through it every day.

That was a turning point for me. And the amazing thing is, this friend is not a talker. But she knew God wanted her to flip her record over in that moment, and she obeyed Him. Without her courage, I might still be overplaying a hit side that was more of a mask.

Are you rotating your record to reveal your flip side? Its contents may be life-changing for another, prompting them to reveal a flip of their own.

—◦—

Keys to Kingdom Living: Courageously share your pain to help others overcome.
Doorpost: "I can do all this though him who gives me strength." Philippians 4:13

DODGING SELF-ESTEEM BARBS: THE ENERGY TRAP

I have a friend I refer to as the Energizer bunny. You may remember this advertising icon from an old battery commercial campaign. The bunny carries a pair of clashing cymbals traveling at a frenetic pace while exhibiting amazing longevity. I always tell her she has two speeds: zero and a hundred and ten. As for me, most days I feel more like the windup toy at the end of a wind. To counteract this tendency, I'm trying to optimize my efficiency, adding little things to my schedule like stepping up the frequency and pace of my exercise routine. By being proactive, I'm combatting the energy trap that's, to some degree, of my own making.

When we're young, we take energy for granted as a renewable resource with vast reserves. But as we get older, our reserves deplete over time and we find ourselves trying to conserve our energy. If you're like me, though, you may have a tendency to beat yourself up if you haven't accomplished your giant to-do list. Who among us hasn't taken one look at a long list and tried to 1) do everything on it and feel defeated when we fail, or 2) take a look at it and pull the covers back over our heads and catch another forty or so winks?

A recent sermon I heard on this very topic addressed doing the things you dread the most first and working your way back to the things you perceive as easier to accomplish. When we embrace this strategy, we are combatting the Enemy's desire to thwart our best intentions. We are told in John 10:10 that the Thief comes "to steal and kill and destroy." His sole purpose is to undermine every good thing you are trying to do in your life. And ours is to thwart him at every turn.

But recognizing his traps is sometimes harder than we think. For instance, we know God wants us to be a good steward with our time. So if we view energy as a currency, we should give careful thought to the value of, say, wasting a day window shopping at stores for things we don't need versus spending it in ways that invest in others. If I decide to go to the mall instead of working on this devotion book, a task the Lord set before me and desires me to complete, I need to ask myself if I have best used my time to further God's kingdom.

That's not to say we aren't free to schedule time for leisure activities. We need to strike a balance of recreation and work so we remain effective and productive without becoming burned out. We should be in constant communication with our Master about how to prioritize our schedules while remaining committed to investing in relationships with family, friends, and those whose lives in our communities we are poised to touch.

—⚮—

Keys to Kingdom Living: Pray for the energy you need to tackle your God-given tasks.
Doorpost: "He gives power to the faint, and to him who has no might he increases strength." Isaiah 40:29 (ESV)

DODGING SELF-ESTEEM BARBS:
TRAPS OF MORTALITY AND AGE

*O*ne of the greatest benefits of my Bible study is the assemblage of women as young as twenty to women well into their nineties. This wide age range fosters an environment of mentorship that has produced a wealth of opportunity in my life to both teach and learn. The younger women are eager to acquire skills and strategies in godly living, while the elder gals enjoy sharing their wisdom with those who are eager to benefit from it.

In this unique group of "Proverbs 31" women, or women who aspire to embody what this infamous passage of the Bible describes, I've been able to see how God uses the willing, and enables them in miraculous ways. I've seen women in their seventies run across a gym floor to get the wiggles out of their young charges before imparting Bible stories to them. I've watched a woman in her eighties spend nine months coaching teenagers to faithfully memorize four pages of Bible verses. I've listened to stories of another in her eighties who enjoys witnessing about Jesus to anyone riding up the ski lift with her, captive to the message she so excitedly wants to deliver.

Biblical figures certainly paved the way with examples of God using the elderly. Noah was 502 years old when he completed the ark and the flood came. Moses was in his eighties when he began his visits to Pharaoh to petition for the release of the Hebrew slaves. Notions of retirement are entirely man-made and not applicable to the Christian life. In fact, as we continue our service, we too are continually transformed. In Proverbs 16:31 we read that "gray hair is a crown of splendor; it is attained in the way of righteousness." Paul said in 1 Timothy 5:17 that the elderly are "worthy of double honor, especially those whose work is preaching and teaching."

Effective Christians all teach to some degree. Ethel Hatfield, at seventy-five, accepted Jesus after years of sitting in church and not quite getting the message. Excited, she went to her bishop and told him she wanted to serve God with the years she had left by teaching Sunday school. The bishop couldn't quite picture her controlling rambunctious youths, so he suggested they pray for direction. The next day she was out in her yard tending roses when a Taiwanese student happened by to ask about her glorious blooms. She invited him in for tea and shared her newfound excitement about Jesus,

The two struck up a friendship and he brought a friend along. Eventually, the group of friends grew to around seventy! These young people, raised in a culture where elders are respected and revered, began coming to her home for Bible study. Many of these young people found Jesus because Ethel didn't let her age didn't hinder her from serving the Lord with her newfound zeal. Rediscover your zeal today!

⊢⸺ᚺ

Keys to Kingdom Living: God never wants us to retire from His kingdom work.

Doorpost: "Worship the Lord your God, and his blessing will be on your food and water. I will take away sickness away from among you . . . I will give you a full life span." Exodus 23:25-26

WEEK 8: WHOPPERS FROM PULPIT AND PEW

WHOPPERS FROM PULPIT AND PEW: GOD WON'T GIVE YOU MORE THAN YOU CAN HANDLE

or centuries, Christians have been approached and challenged by unbelievers with what I call the hard questions. These include the gut-wrenching—how can a loving God let a child die—to the horrific—can God really exist in a world where the Holocaust was permitted to occur? These hard questions are heaped onto a pile of atrocities we can't understand. Even Christians struggle with these paradoxes from time to time. But bigger problems arise when tough talk like this is met with a barrage of pat responses cloaked in misused Bible verses.

What's more frustrating to suffering unbelievers than placating replies to raw, emotionally charged inquiries? The single most infuriating response I continue to receive when someone learns I have an autistic child is, "Well God never gives you more than you can handle." My thought when I hear this is twofold: (1) they have no earthly idea what walking a mile in my shoes feels like, and (2) saying this completely discounts any pain and suffering on my part. This dismissal is, at the very least, unhelpful, and at its worst is cruel and unloving. Invalidating an unbeliever's feelings when they ask a hard question will only further distance them from the possibility of a come-to-Jesus moment.

Well-meaning, albeit misguided, people invoke the "no more than you can handle" comment based on the passage in 1

Corinthians 10:13, which addresses being able to bear up under temptation—not hardship. Temptation is different from a burden. When Jesus was in the garden of Gethsemane, He didn't wipe away the sweat drops of blood. He didn't minimize his situation with a platitude. He confessed His anguish in prayer and asked God to "remove this cup," completing His prayer with "Your will be done," and followed through, according to Luke 22:42.

When Paul wrote of his hardships in Asia in 2 Corinthians chapter 1, he relayed an honest account of a load of sufferings that went so far beyond their strength that they were afraid they might not survive. David talked of being "worn out, utterly crushed" in Psalms 38:8 (GNT). Truth be told, the Enemy would love you to believe that if you feel like you're being crushed under your burden, something's wrong with you and you don't have enough faith, or you wouldn't be in such an awful spot.

There are two important facts to consider here. One is that, while God will rule and reign in the New Jerusalem, Satan's time to conquer, divide, and wreak havoc is now. In our broken world there are plenty of unbearable situations that some people can handle and some can't on this side of eternity. Things like terminal illness, addiction, and suicidal thoughts are a few examples. In excruciatingly painful situations like these, we need to cling to God's promises for ourselves and stifle our comments and judgment regarding others who didn't bear up under them. Only God fully knows our hearts.

⊢•—◦

Keys to Kingdom Living: Acknowledging hard questions is preferable and far more helpful than dispensing platitudes.
Doorpost: "Cast all your anxiety on Him because He cares for you." 1 Peter 5:7

WHOPPERS FROM PULPIT AND PEW:
PRAY HARD ENOUGH, GOD WILL
ANSWER YOUR WAY

Back in 1971, singer Janis Joplin recorded a song with the famous chorus line, "Oh, Lord, won't you buy me a Mercedes Benz," adding to the petition a color TV and a night on the town.[1] Of course, it's easy to see by this "prayer" that Janis wasn't exactly fervently praying for God's will with her wish list for shots of liquor and adult toys.

Christians who enjoy a rich and rewarding relationship with their Father God have moved beyond Christmas-list prayers, likely to enjoy a more fulfilling prayer life. But the intimacy of communication and the sincerity of the petitioner doesn't necessarily equate with our desired answer and a rousing testimony. Though there are several verses in the Bible that proclaim we will receive what we want when we pray, these verses are not intended to be promises. They are meant to encourage us to talk to God honestly about what we think we want and need. Sometimes we will receive our heart's desire, but it is always up to Him to decide if we do in the final analysis. God doesn't want us to pray to Him so He can dispense what's on our list. He's the Most High God, not our Santa Claus.

When I was twelve, and long, flowing hair was all the rage, I asked my parents for a "fall," the name for a long wig in those days. My mother kept trying to talk me out of it, saying that it would look unnatural and that I really wouldn't like the way it looked on me. Still, I begged and pleaded. On Christmas Day, I opened a box—and to my surprise, there it was. When I wore it to school, everyone laughed. Naturally, I was mortified. That was my first experience with getting something I wanted that wasn't at all what I needed!

God has our back. He knows what is best for us even when we don't, and He answers every prayer based on the plans and purposes for our lives that only He knows. Back in 2007, when my husband and I were looking for a new house, we bid on a home that was near foreclosure. It was pretty beat up inside. The owner had stripped out the wires, and we wouldn't have been able to bring our autistic son there for many months while we restored it. The deal fell through. Perplexed, I went to the Lord in prayer, and He said to me, "That's not God's best for you." Two months later, we found a better house for a lower price, and I understood then that God heard me and answered differently.

Naturally, God has not answered all my prayers in the way I have wanted. My twenty-year-old is non-verbal, though I've prayed hard and long for recovery. But as God showed me with the house that got away, He has different plans for Max and for me. He wants me to love him unconditionally. He wants me to authentically share my struggles with autism and other issues on these pages to encourage you as you persevere in your own struggles. The success of a prayer should not be measured by outcome but by how we humbly submit to His answer. He will "make all things new" in eternity, if not here on earth.

Keys to Kingdom Living: Pray knowing God's answer may differ from your desire.

Doorpost: "Then you will call upon me and come and pray to me, and I will listen to you." Jeremiah 29:12

WHOPPERS FROM PULPIT AND PEW:
CHRISTIANS SHOULD BE HAPPY

Happiness as a goal and life mission continues to be celebrated in everything from popular songs and ads to texting emoticons. Catch phrases such as "don't worry, be happy" might be fine to listen to as we drive around in our cars. But in doing real life, pretending to be happy all the time makes everyone, including Christians, look more like robots than human beings trying to bring salt and light to a predominately unhappy world.

While it's true that many a Bible verse speaks of a joy that should be contagious to non-Christians, it is at times inappropriate and often inauthentic to display cheerfulness and talk of happiness. For instance, we can be happy in our hearts that a Christian has gone on to their eternal reward, but we wouldn't necessarily bring a handful of forty balloons to the memorial service and rush into the sanctuary bursting with exuberance, saddling up to the survivors who just lost their loved one. A more heartfelt response would be a warm hug and a reassuring, sincere verbal acknowledgment of their pain and loss.

I remember reading a disturbing account in a Christian book about an Ethiopian pastor. He was conducting a service when Communist government officials burst in to stop the "illegal" proceedings. When the people refused to halt the service, one of the solders grabbed the minister's three-year-old baby girl and threw her out the third story window. The author goes on to say that the mother ran down, retrieved the girl, and cradled her dead baby in her arms in her front row seat as the service continued. There is nothing in his account of people surrounding her in prayer or any reports of crying, but only about how they carried on.

While I understand the point of this story is to illustrate that the enemies of God will not be defeated, if it were true that the poor baby's mother stifled her emotions to help prove the point —which I find very hard to believe—what does that say to others? It says we are callous and unfeeling towards the terrible things that happen in life or that we exhibit a fake public persona not to be trusted. If the author left out such pertinent information to illustrate that we must carry on without showing emotion no matter what the cost, I can't in good faith condone what appears disingenuous and improbable.

We are told in Ecclesiastes 3 that there is a season for everything. Verses 3 and 4 say there is "a time to tear down and a time to build, a time to weep and a time to laugh, a time to mourn and a time to dance." When a baby—or anyone—dies, we don't dance. We need to honor seasons in our own lives and in the lives of others as they run their course. And when others come to us and bare their souls, sharing their pain and grief as you sit with them in the moment, such outpourings should not be met with Bible verses about joy. Instead, take the opportunity to give the gift of listening to show deep love. By doing this, you honor Christ's commandment of loving them as Christ loved you (Matthew 22:39).

—●●—

Keys to Kingdom Living: False joy is no advertisement for Christianity and is an inappropriate response to unfortunate circumstances, tragedies, and disasters.
Doorpost: "Bear one another's burdens and so fulfill the law of Christ." Galatians 6:2 (ESV)

WHOPPERS FROM PULPIT AND PEW:
EVERYTHING THAT HAPPENS
ORIGINATES FROM GOD'S PLAN

This phrase may ring true in a broad sense, but when we apply it to individual events, it becomes less accurate and less helpful in navigating life's difficulties in our broken world. We don't have the benefit of looking back on our life from end to beginning. God doesn't always bring about resolution as we would like it to unfold on this side of eternity.

The account of Job's life in the Old Testament provides a solid example of how God can work with tragedies to accomplish good. We remember from chapters 1 and 2 in this famous book of the Bible that it is Satan who comes to God with the idea to test Job. Satan suggests that because Job enjoyed great favor, his love for God had never been tested. So under God's watch, but not by His hand, Satan was given permission to wreak havoc in Job's life.

As Job was tested, his seven sons and three daughters were taken from him. He lost his 7,000 sheep, 3,000 camels, 500 pairs of oxen, 500 female donkeys, and many servants. Described in Job 1:3 as "the greatest man among the all the people of the East" in terms of personal wealth, Job found himself so painfully ill that his wife encouraged him to curse God and die. But Job doesn't blame God or chalk it up to any plan. He doesn't sugarcoat his circumstances, either. He is honest and forthright about his condition, stating, "I loathe my life. I will give free utterance to my complaint," in chapter 10, verse 1

(ESV). Job does acknowledge that God has wisdom and might as well as counsel and understanding, and continues to exhibit integrity throughout his ordeal.

Eventually, God restores Job and gives him twice as much as he had before. But you won't find passages in Job that say the replenishment negated the losses incurred in his trial. It was a very real cost to lose his seven sons and three daughters, even though God gave him seven new sons and three new daughters. We are told in chapter 42, verse 11, that his close relatives and friends showed him sympathy and comforted him for all the evil the Lord permitted Satan to heap on him. They didn't say "it was all part of God's plan" in order to try to dismiss the suffering he endured. They properly acknowledged what he had gone through and rejoiced with him when it was over. God used what happened to Job and bought good out of that adversity.

Evil shapes our destiny. Evil people can still be involved in the ultimate plans of God. And our free will to choose can also alter our course. But God can transform the chaos of personal and peripheral circumstances in our lives and still use them for His higher plans and purposes. That's where Romans 8:28 really shows its muscle: God works within the framework of your choices and still accomplishes a plan for you. Focusing on the effect of a trial as pain and loss alone neglects to take into consideration the gain of spiritual growth. At the end of the day, that is the holy grail of the Christian walk.

━━•⊱

Keys to Kingdom Living: God may permit evil or bad choices, but He isn't the direct cause of them.
Doorpost: "And we know that for those who love God all things work together for good, for those who are called according to His purposes." Romans 8:28 (ESV)

WHOPPERS FROM PULPIT AND PEW:
THE LORD HELPS THOSE WHO HELP
THEMSELVES

*In luxury hotels in Dubai, vending machines stocked with solid gold bars amuse bored guests. But in sharp contrast, in neighboring Sonapur, thousands of workers from India, Pakistan, Bangladesh, and China are vastly underpaid and live in squalor.

In the fancy Upper East Side neighborhood in Manhattan, on Park Avenue, high rises are filled with hedge fund managers who are living in the lap of luxury. Yet slightly to the northeast, on the other side of the Harlem River, the Park Avenue that's in South Bronx is home to America's poorest congressional district. There in South Bronx, about 40 percent of the residents, many of them unemployed, make less than $40 a day. The disparity is staggering.

In California where I live, it's not uncommon to see a home-less person pushing a shopping cart past Lamborghinis in the parking lot of a local supermarket. It's in these moments where the "haves" come in direct contact with the "have-nots." Some needs are greater than others. I've spoken with the young home-less man who refuses the drip coffee I offer to buy him as I stand in line to buy my own drip at Starbucks. He politely declines, stating that he's going to instead hold out for a triple latte. Since I'm not a $7 cup of coffee kind of consumer, he will wait for what he wants. But I've also looked into the eyes of a homeless woman holding her baby daughter and, seeing her fear and true need, given her money. But the more I come in contact with the have-nots, the more I learn the *why* and *how* are far less important than my response in the face of genuine need.

I've told these stories to others and have heard, time and time again, the comment "the Lord helps those who help themselves." As much as this might sound like a proverb of Solomon, this sentence isn't anywhere in the Bible. The idea behind it is misconstrued from the verses where Paul states, the one who is unwilling to work "neither should he eat" (2 Thessalonians 3:10). This verse was mean to communicate that whoever was able-bodied was expected to pull his weight so as not to be a burden to the others who were also contributing in their community. Paul is clearly speaking here to those who have the ability and opportunity to work. He's not talking about the disabled, or about those who look for work and cannot find it. He is not referring to people who are too old, those responsible for young charges or older parents, or those with obsolete jobs or skills in our changing world.

Truth be told, the Lord actually blesses those who help others. He even commands it: "love one another" are words Jesus spoke in John 34:35 that clearly trump circumstances when someone has a need that's not being met. I do pray for discernment when someone asks for help but also remind myself of this: "People look at the outward appearance, but the Lord looks at the heart" (1 Samuel 16:7).

—◦—

Keys to Kingdom Living: We are responsible to help the truly needy among us.
Doorpost: "For there will never cease to be poor in the land. Therefore I command you, you shall open wide your hand to your brother, to the needy and to the poor, in your land." Deuteronomy 15:11 (ESV)

WHOPPERS FROM PULPIT AND PEW:
SACRED VS. SECULAR

On the first Sunday I served in student ministries at my church, I arrived early as the musicians were setting up their gear for the morning worship. Over the loudspeaker, the youth minister punched in a playlist with pop songs on it. At first I was somewhat surprised that he didn't choose a more sacred playlist. But when I realized he had carefully chosen the songs so words and subject matter did not offend, I realized that the peppy beat was intended to help get the work done quickly, which it did. There was nothing inappropriate about carefully chosen non-sacred music in a church environment.

Sometimes as Christians we tend to overplay what is sacred and run amok with the concept. We see in James 1:27 where we are to keep the world from contaminating us. And Paul rightly says in Philippians 4 that we should think about things that are pure, true, and noble. We are indeed sanctified and made holy by the blood of the Lamb. We are a royal priesthood, a holy nation. But not everything that isn't blessed in a sacrament or connected to church is bad and needs to be avoided. I remember a particularly funny example of the secular and sacred coming together. At the conservative Protestant church I grew up in, my mother was in charge of the altar guild. One Sunday, when communion was scheduled, the pastor told my mother that they had run out of wine and that she needed to go out and get some. "But doesn't the wine come from church headquarters where it's blessed?" she asked. The pastors had a laugh and then told her she could just run down to the liquor store and pick it up. The wine was ordinary to begin with and became sacred only after it was blessed. In the same way, the lambs used in sacrifices in the Old Testament were ordinary until they were later set apart for God.

Sacred and secular things indeed often occupy the same field at some point; what differs is for what purpose an object is used. Pop music is played to energize and awaken sleepy band members at 6:30 a.m. on a Sunday when "Amazing Grace" might not do the job. Conversely, Ku Klux Klan members hold a cross as they burn down an African-American church; they carry the very symbol of forgiveness, grace, and inclusion, though their mission is far from God-pleasing. In these cases, there is nothing sacred about the cross or secular about the pop music. Arbitrarily labeling objects and practices is simplistic and misleading.

We are told we are "set apart," in Deuteronomy 14:2. But that's God's doing. What might be a more effective method of setting ourselves apart than labeling sacred and secular? Remembering that our bodies contain the Most High God! We are told in Galatians 2:20 that Christ lives *in us*. If we keep this in mind as we use the objects in this world to accomplish His plans and purposes (or even just to have some fun from time to time without undermining them), we can realize we don't need to cloak everything in nobility. We are told in 1 Timothy 6:17 that God "richly provides us with everything for our enjoyment."

Keys to Kingdom Living: Sacred and secular needn't be diametrically opposed.
Doorpost: "Whether you eat or drink, or whatever you do, do it all for the glory of God." 1 Corinthians 10:31

WHOPPERS FROM PULPIT AND PEWS;
ALL RELIGIONS LEAD TO GOD

*U*nlike almost all the other false notions we've examined in this seven-day series, the idea that all religions lead to God doesn't come from a misconstrued Bible verse. The Bible is full of verses about the one true God. Some religions are born of misguided inclusions to Biblical foundations; others are wrapped in the blanket of tolerance that permeates a worldview that is not in line with the Bible in its entirety. It's not uncommon to hear the uniformed or the duped say that all searches for a higher being lead to God.

Christians recognize the unique lynchpin of their faith in the Being for whom there has not been nor ever will be any equal: Jesus Christ. Historically, no other religion devoid of Christ has ever claimed that their divine one rose from the grave to conquer death. Any other roads that others may claim lead to a god that is equal to Jesus (or somehow basically the same) don't line up with the one true path Christians know they must take. Any claimants insisting that the roads are the same are gravely mistaken. But in a world where tolerance is revered more than strong convictions, it's becoming harder and harder to refute the "all roads" concept among non-believers. It's a trap we'd do well to avoid.

Scripture is clear: Jesus says He is the only way. He tells us this in John chapter 10. We read verse 7 that He is the door for us as "sheep," and he said earlier in verse 1 that "anyone who does not enter the sheepfold by the gate, but climbs in by some other way, is a thief and a robber." Christians not only need to be wary of any stray paths we come in contact with, we need to pay attention to the paths of those who surround us, even in casual ways, so we too are not deceived. As the end times approach, this will be even an even more important aspect of our discernment.

I was once a part of a discussion in which I was presented with a new method of refuting this notion. The person, a believer, was discussing an encounter she'd had with a non-believer who stated their "all roads" opinion to my Christian friend. Instead of simply arguing the point, my friend simply stated that it didn't matter at all what she herself thought; what mattered to her was what God said. My friend went on to say that she was in no position to argue with God, despite her feelings.

Of course, we need to discern through prayer whether or not an "all roads" disagreement could result in an intervention of the Holy Spirit and a potential conversion. What we never want to do is be tempted to fall into this line of faulty thinking ourselves. Our best hedge against watering down our beliefs is to continually renew our own minds with God's holy Word and its solid truths, entirely unworthy of dilution.

⊢⟶ᴓ

Keys to Kingdom Living: There's only one door that leads to salvation: Jesus!
Doorpost: "I am the way, the truth and the life. No one comes to the Father except through me." John 14:6 (NKJV)

WEEK 9: LEARNING FROM WOMEN OF THE BIBLE

LEARNING FROM THE WOMEN OF THE BIBLE: EVE AND THE TRAP OF SUPERIORITY

*E*ve was the first scapegoat. The fall of mankind was pinned on her ever since she bit into the succulent forbidden fruit. First, it was her husband blaming her before God. Today, generations later, people still point the finger at the woman who sold out Paradise.

We can learn a great deal from Eve's break with God, even if we aren't always willing to admit that we would have fallen for the same trap were we the one standing in the sunny garden, engaged in seemingly casual conversation with the Prince of Darkness. Eve, unlike us, didn't have the benefit of God's holy Word. She wasn't well-versed on putting on the armor of God (Ephesians 6:11). She didn't know she was no match for the Devil's arguments and that fleeing from him would have been her wisest course of action.

The seeds of pride proved to be the beginning of her downfall. As the serpent conversed with Eve, Satan offered up well-crafted half-truths, distorting God's words to entice her to deduce that she knew better than God did. Instead of fleeing, she wrongly pondered Satan's flawed reasoning. Then, thinking for herself, she fell victim to the visual temptation. We read in Genesis 3:6 that Eve "saw that the tree was good for food, and that it was a delight to the eyes," and that it would "make one wise" (ESV), so she succumbed to the temptation of eating one piece of forbidden fruit in the middle of an orchard of acceptable choices.

You might be thinking to yourself, why did she need that one piece of fruit when she had her choice among so many? But think about it: how often do we reach for the "forbidden fruit"? When we stand at the salad bar with over fifty kinds of sliced raw vegetables, why does the chocolate pudding look so appealing? Why does the man married to a beautiful and faithful wife reach for one-dimensional pornography when his three-dimensional soul mate resides under the same roof? It is precisely because human beings are highly prone to falling into disobedience.

You might have heard it said that none of us drift toward obedience. If we are honest, we admit we don't always make the sound choice. Of the over million plus words in the English language, do we always choose those that edify God, or do occasional vulgarities and slurs creep into our vocabularies? Do we always pursue the lost sheep in a sea of believers at church each week, or have we been known to duck them because our crowded agenda won't permit one more interruption? We not only can learn from Eve's mistakes but can be assured of God's plan to redeem us from our disobedience.

⊶

Keys to Kingdom Living: Learn from Eve's mistakes and flee from dialog with Satan and his temptations.
Doorpost: "Submit yourselves, then, to God. Resist the devil, and he will flee from you." James 4:7

LEARNING FROM WOMEN OF THE BIBLE: LOT'S WIFE AND THE TRAP OF DISOBEDIENCE

*ot's wife's fall from grace is a tragic cautionary tale. She went from respected wife of the last godly patriarch on earth to reluctant pilgrim to what one writer of ancient text referred to as "a monument of an unbelieving soul."

Her ordeal began as God reached His breaking point regarding Sodom and Gomorrah. He'd decided to destroy the wicked cities but spare Lot's family by relocating them to another nearby town. When the time came for the exodus, the angels leading them out very clearly told Lot, his wife, and their two daughters in Genesis 19 to flee or be swept away when Sodom and Gomorrah were destroyed. Most importantly, they were told not to look back under any circumstances. Sadly, Lot's wife was unable to obey that last command. I doubt that she turned her head immediately in direct defiance with God's edict. But in a moment of weakness, she couldn't resist doing just that.

Lot's wife's misstep serves as an example of what not to do when the ultimate day of reckoning comes as well. Jesus reminds his disciples. In Luke 17:29, Jesus recounts the element of surprise associated with the day Sodom and Gomorrah was destroyed.

"It will be just like this on the day the Son of Man is revealed. On that day, no one who is on the housetop, with possessions inside,

should go down to get them. Likewise, no one in the field should go back for anything. Remember Lot's wife!"

One of the most interesting aspects of this story lies in its ambiguity. We aren't told in Scripture why Lot's wife looked back. The first time I read this story, I thought she may have been reticent to leave her stuff behind. Now I realize the story is undoubtedly more powerful with the motive left unsaid. Readers can interpret for themselves what it might have been, possibly letting light into the window of their own psyche and the kinds of things that might have caused their own heads to turn. What kinds of things tempt you to take your eyes off of God's leadings in your life?

We must keep our eyes on Jesus, no matter where He leads us and no matter what sacrifices we are asked to make to do so. For Lot's wife, leaving behind all she knew, and could see, for something unknown and yet unseen proved too much. We need to trust God's promises about all He has prepared for us. In Joel 2:25, we are told that God will repay us for the years the locusts have eaten our crops. God will right every wrong. We can count on Him to wield His impartial justice. We learn in Matthew 16:25 that "whoever wants to save their life will lose it, but whoever loses their life for [Jesus] will find it." Lot's wife had no way of knowing these truths or that of Luke 12:33-34, where we read of the treasure in heaven that cannot be stolen by thieves or eaten by moths: "For where your treasure is, your heart will be also." Lot's wife couldn't leave her earthly treasure entirely behind. May we be able to pass that test.

—⚷—

Keys to Kingdom Living: Don't let anything take your eyes off God's divine direction.
Doorpost: "Let your eyes look straight ahead; fix your gaze directly before you." Proverbs 4:25

LEARNING FROM WOMEN OF THE BIBLE: SARAH AND THE TRAP OF BYPASSING GOD'S PLAN

*U*ntil you've known the pain of infertility or been close to someone who has suffered in this way, it's hard to understand how deeply some situations can wound. I know this pain firsthand and remember when I declined baby shower invites and avoided meeting with my young mom friends with their darling children in tow. At my lowest, I even skipped church on Mother's Day and made my husband bring me to a biker bar for lunch where the chances of seeing moms and their young charges were slim to none!

Sarah, the wife of the promised father of many nations, knew that same pain. The road mapped out for her this side of eternity was filled with several decades of deep disappointment. Though she and her husband enjoyed great wealth and abundance, they remained childless well into their golden years. She endured her childlessness for as long as she felt she was able. However, Sarah's greatest misstep was her attempt to circumvent God's plan and His perfect timing. She persuaded Hagar, her servant girl, to have sex with her husband so he could father a child. She convinced Abraham to go along with the plan.

Despite the couple's ill-conceived plan, God still followed through His promise to make Abraham the father of many nations—but even as God spoke to reiterate it, Sarah overheard Him inside her tent and laughed. God's response was not of anger. Instead, He responded rhetorically, "Is anything too hard for God?" Of course, the answer to God's rhetorical question was "absolutely not!"

However, the circumvention of God's plan made their lives harder and even changed history. By hatching their own scheme instead of trusting in God, their action resulted in a situation that God still used for good but caused a great deal of heartache, especially for Hagar and for her son named Ishmael. Though Ishmael was not an heir to the promise as his half-brother Isaac was, Ishmael still enjoyed a promise made by God to bless him, which God did. However, the existence of Ishmael alongside Jacob set the stage for the animosity between Jews and Muslims that is still harbored today.

The reason it is so hard to trust God when we don't have all the facts is the same reason why it's so important we do just that. How often do we think we know better than God? We say to ourselves that He simply doesn't understand our life. But again we find another paradox: no one understands it better than He does! We can learn from Sarah's mistake to leapfrog over God's plan by instead adopting the infamous FROG principle: Fully Relying On God. When we do, we can be sure of remaining rooted in His will and trusting in His perfect promises.

—⸖—

Keys to Kingdom Living: Trust God in all you do and in all your circumstances, instead of compartmentalizing your trust, and you will enjoy the blessed assurance of right relationship with God.

Doorpost: "For nothing is impossible with God." Luke 1:37 (NLT)

LEARNING FROM WOMEN OF THE BIBLE: ESTHER AND THE VICTORY OVER THE TRAP OF FEAR

The dramatic book of Esther is as riveting as it is educational. Beauty queen metamorphoses into real queen, accepts the responsibility of securing her people's preservation while eliminating a national enemy, and exemplifies what it means to be a great wife and life partner.

The many lessons we can learn from someone as amazing as Esther wouldn't begin to fit on this page. Her character, actions, and words speak volumes, as does one of the most famous verses from the book of the Bible written about her, namely, "And who knows but that you have come to your royal position for such as time as this?" (Esther 4:14). Esther faced a divine appointment within the confines of her unique opportunity to wield influence for the greater good. She revealed the assassination plot on the king and helped foil the plot of Haman to eradicate the Jewish people and, subsequently, Esther herself. When Esther went to live in the palace, she surely had no idea of the opportunity she would find herself in to be of service to anyone but the king himself.

We too have daily, even hourly opportunities to serve our King. We may be asked to give to the needy, reach out in friendship to the lonely, or advocate for those who can't speak for themselves. When we do, we are able to wield our influence.

I often attend meetings for my developmentally disabled son, and I like to bring a picture of him along. He's nonverbal and cannot advocate for himself. His image reminds others of his "personhood." You might be surprised at how few people actually have his best interests at heart. God's been very clear to charge me with that responsibility and the importance of it, especially since he cannot speak for himself. We are told in Proverbs 31:8 to "speak up for those who cannot speak for themselves; ensure justice for those being crushed" (NLT). Esther worked hard to understand the law of the land at a time when women were far from encouraged to undertake scholarly pursuits. She discerned in her unique situation that breaking man's law might be necessary for the preservation of her people.

Divine appointments aside, probably the most striking lesson learned from Esther lies in her tremendous courage. We read her powerful declaration of self-sacrifice in Esther 4:16, when she defies law to accomplish her objective: "I will go to the king, even though it is against the law. And if I perish, I perish."

Like Jesus, we may be called into precarious situations to accomplish kingdom assignments. When I traveled to Rwanda, I knew malaria and nearby warfare were real threats. But as Jesus said whoever loves his life loses it, and whoever hates his life in this world will keep it for all eternity. We must decide whether we'll live for Jesus's plans and purposes or tick off the hours with our own self-preservation in mind.

Keys to Kingdom Living: Display the courage of Esther to enhance effectiveness in your own life.
Doorpost: "Be strong and courageous." Deuteronomy 31:6

LEARNING FROM WOMEN OF THE BIBLE: MARY AND THE VICTORY OVER THE TRAP OF APPEARANCE

*B*eing the mother of Jesus may sound like the greatest honor a woman could have in the history of mankind, but that celestial honor didn't come without an earthly price. The virgin birth of Jesus was not exactly understood, even though it was revealed in Isaiah that a virgin would conceive and bear a son and call Him Immanuel.

With Mary's betrothal to Joseph, and the speed with which they were wed, those who were not privy to the details of Gabriel's news might have wondered about Mary's pre-wedding virginity. With the exception of Joseph and Zechariah to whom the truth was revealed, we don't read anything in Scripture that suggests anyone else believed Jesus was the promised Messiah, including Mary's parents or even the siblings of Jesus.

I believe the reason for this is that Mary in particular, and Joseph to some degree, were chosen for their willingness to sacrifice a great deal to accomplish the work they were born to undertake. Jesus Himself sacrificed His own life as a ransom for many as we learn in Matthew 20:28. We read in Matthew 1:18 that Mary was found to be with child from the Holy Spirit before she and Joseph united as man and wife. Both Joseph and Mary, undoubtedly people of high moral character, suddenly found themselves the subject of a great deal of gossip and speculation. Their character and reputations were being called into question based on appearances and speculation they did not deserve.

Many renowned, invaluable servants of God were subject to ridicule and maligning. Carpenter Noah was laughed at, as was the childless father of many nations, Abraham. Dreamer Joseph was entrapped and sold into slavery, and diminutive warrior David was laughed at before he flattened Goliath. We read nowhere of these great men lamenting over the unjust hand they were dealt, but only of their obedience and love for their Father God. The same is true of Mary. Instead of whining about what her friends or family were going to think, she embraced her destiny with zeal rather than resignation. Her beautiful recitation we call the Magnificat (which you can read in Luke 1:46-55) reveals her humble acceptance of the honor bestowed on her, shifting the glory and honor off of her and on to her Creator.

Mary relinquishes public opinion while enduring the seemingly unbearable sacrifice of losing her son to an unjustifiable, excruciating death by crucifixion. Her courageous presence at the cross, her amazing ability to stand strong to the end of her precious son's life, is as incomprehensible to me as it may be to you. Next time we're called to endure pain during a perceived injustice, we would do well to follow Mary's example of obedience and strength in the face of her unimaginable adversity.

⊢⊷β⊷

Keys to Kingdom Living: Obey God with zeal no matter what the personal cost.
Doorpost: "For behold, from now on all generations will call me blessed for the mighty one has done great things for me." Luke 1:48-49

LEARNING FROM WOMEN OF THE BIBLE: THE WOMAN AT THE WELL AND THE TRAP OF SHAME

*T*he redemptive story of the woman at the well serves as a powerful reminder of the profound impact of a compelling testimony. In fact, any testimony that turns a person's life around is compelling to those who know them Such is the case with the woman at the well.

It is perhaps fitting that we don't know her name. To some degree, we are all "her." Every once-lost sinner embodies her characteristics. Before we are saved, our sins are piled high like an untended garbage heap. When Jesus meets her and asks her to assist in getting Him a drink of water, she's inclined to believe He doesn't have a clue who she is—yet she soon receives the surprise of her life in the form of a thumbnail dossier of her past.

When she informs Him she is a Samaritan, she implies He might not have known. (Historically, Jews were to have nothing to do with speaking or fraternizing with residents of Samaria, because Jews considered Samaritans to be of mixed blood and therefore not Jewish in the pure sense of the word. Jesus conceded this and then laid out her past regarding her four previous husbands and her current live-in paramour. When He finally reveals His identity as the Messiah, she not only takes the leap of faith, she runs to the townspeople to tell everyone about Jesus and who she believes He is.

How inclined are we to tell everyone about Jesus? Do we

keep such talk alive in comfortable circles of believers, where we know the truth will be accepted? Or are we, like the woman at the well, willing to risk ridicule and judgment as we tell our tale? By even going to the town, she was paying a price by risking outright rejection. She had made it a point to go to the well midday, when few women would make the journey, isolating herself on purpose. But isn't it just like Jesus to plan to keep the divine appointment we have no idea we'll be thrust into?

Instead of remaining withdrawn, she not only ran into town, she left her water jar behind. The woman at the well, having already received her "living water," eagerly went to tell the townspeople about Jesus. We read in John 4 that they not only left town and went to the well to come to him, but that many from the town believed in Him because of the woman's testimony.

How many will come to believe because of *your* testimony? Are you willing to leave your water jar behind to tell of what God has done for you? Are you eager to share what redemption has meant to you by turning your selfish life around in service to Him? Or are you afraid of admitting old mistakes, however redeemed, in front of others? It's true that there's a cost in every testimony when we admit past wrongdoing. But every time we do it, we invest in someone who could be forever changed after hearing what you alone have to say. Will you spend that currency?

Keys to Kingdom Living: Drop everything to "go tell it on the mountain."

Doorpost: "For I am not ashamed of the gospel, for it is the power of God for salvation to everyone who believes." Romans 1:16 (NASB)

LEARNING FROM WOMEN OF THE BIBLE: MARY MAGDALENE AND THE PATH OF UNABASHED DEVOTION

*P*erhaps no biblical figure is as misunderstood or mis-written about as Mary Magdalene. Films and websites riddled with false information are primarily to blame. She's been falsely portrayed as a former prostitute, speculated about as a paramour of Jesus, and misidentified as the woman who wept over Jesus's feet and anointed them with expensive perfume.

If truth is to be told, we don't know much about Mary Magdalene other than the fact that Jesus released her from seven demons as recorded in Luke 8. But, like Mary, we've been healed of our demons as well. Any Christian knows that a powerful encounter with Jesus resulting in a genuine life change remains a hallmark of their life until the day we are to be reunited with Him. Until then, like Mary, we can and ought to devote our lives to Him as she did.

We might possibly be able to discern, based on what we read in Luke 8, that Mary, along with two other women named with Joanna and Susanna, provided for Jesus's ministry out of their means. It may seem like a stretch that women of the day would have any means at all other than what their husbands provided. But we learn in Proverbs 31 of the ideal woman of an industrious nature who ran several enterprises to the glory of God.

When we invest any resource in the work of the Lord, we genuinely glorify and serve Him. Whether we give money, time, or talent, all of these gifts require some sacrifice on our part that will be pleasing to the Lord. Mary Magdalene certainly gave of her time and sacrificed her comfort as well. She stood with Mary the mother of Jesus at the foot of the bloody cross. She went with Mary the wife of Clopas, Salome, and the mother of James and John to the tomb of Jesus to bring spices.

We learn in Mark 16:9 that Jesus appeared first after His glorious resurrection to Mary Magdalene. In stark contrast to the famous skirmish in Luke 9:46 among the disciples over which was the greatest, Jesus chose not one of the twelve as His first resurrection witness but a woman, She was on a mission. She exhibited a true and pure servant's heart. Before hearing and seeing the miracle of Him standing there in front of her, she was weeping uncontrollably. Even though Mary ran to tell the tale to the other apostles, we read in Luke 24:11 that her words seemed to them an "idle tale," and they did not believe any of it. (Well, at least not initially).

We can choose, like Mary, to devote our time, talents, and financial resources to expanding God's kingdom. We can honor God in service by rolling up our sleeves to do the work He's laid out for us in this life. Finally, we can recognize the blessings God gives us as He reveals Himself to us in His truths, His glory, and His plan for our lives. We can devote ourselves to living for Him in the present and beyond as we look forward to the day of restoration.

Keys to Kingdom Living: Devote all you have to further your precious Redeemer's kingdom.
Doorpost: "Only fear the LORD and serve him faithfully with all your heart; consider what great things he has done for you." 1 Samuel 12:24

WEEK 10: COVERT GARDENING

COVERT GARDENING: TENDING
UNPACKED

*T*he first time I witnessed the groundwork for covert gardening, I discovered a new kind of divine intervention. *Covert gardening* involves praying to the Creator for my desired outcome to a situation involving someone else. I use prayer about someone else without speaking directly to that person about a hot button issue. I avoid directly trying to cultivate the soil of the person being prayed for with my own verbal input. In doing this, I surrender my drama of picking up the pitchfork and stirring up the soil myself. I surrender . . . and let God do the work. By doing this, I'm able to give up a puffed-up attitude and statements like, "This crummy soil needs so much help, and here I am again trying to make something out of it, as only I can do."

Secretive gardening replaces more public corporate or group prayer in situations requiring heightened discretion and delicacy. In those kinds of situations, public prayer might be appropriate and well-intended in its delivery but could produce a "return to sender" reaction on the part of the recipient. Out loud, some prayer might come across more as disapproval. Even the noblest of efforts are rarely well received by the subject in those kinds of cases, especially when it involves something that they themselves might not want to come to pass even when the prayer warrior does.

Effective covert gardening encompasses the notion that

praying for that person is more effective than badgering them to change. We, as praying Christians, can do that for the people we love without standing on a soapbox and pontificating. Talking about gardening never produces tangible results. It is in the act of gardening itself where the environments can be transformed. Just as the empty words "I'll pray for you" are meaningless without the action itself, the person who neglects to follow through with genuine prayer and petition after agreeing to do it hasn't accomplished a thing regardless of intent or proclamation.

As with regular gardening, we must be consistent in our efforts. In the book *The Secret Garden* by Francis Hodgson Burnett, a neglected garden was transformed over an extended time. Persistence and consistency are key components. We can't just water our garden when it occurs to us. It needs water daily to achieve optimum results. We must pray to the Holy Spirit for His living water to freshly anoint the person or situation. The garden also needs access to sun—or the Son. Pray for a "come-to-Jesus moment" for that situation or person and godly mentors for the person or for enrichment of the situation's landscape. Ask for God's will in each matter.

⊶⊶

Keys to Kingdom Living: Tend your secret gardens with authentic prayer and petition.
Doorpost: "In simple humility, let our gardener God landscape you with the Word." James 1:21 (MSG)

COVERT GARDENING: GLOBAL GARDENING

*W*hen it comes to current events and international matters, covert gardening serves a unique purpose. When we feel frustrated and helpless over the increasingly alarming situations plaguing our troubled world, sitting around lamenting or complaining does little, if anything, to facilitate real change. And it's not like Russian president Vladimir Putin or North Korean dictator Kim Jong-un will be taking your calls anytime soon.

Thankfully, God always takes your call. He will listen to your frustrations over injustices in our world. He cares for our hurts and worries, as we learn in 1 Peter 5:7. In fact, in 1 Timothy 2:2, Paul reminds us to pray for all who are in authority so we can live peaceful and quiet lives. What better place to lay down your global burden than at the feet of Jesus?

Persistence should remain a hallmark of the prayer warrior. We should regularly pray for the poor and oppressed, victims of human trafficking, child soldiers, Christian mission teams, persecuted Christians, the wrongly incarcerated, our military members engaged in tours of duty, victims of terrorist acts, slave laborers, and even the perpetrators of these inhumane acts. I'm becoming more and more aware of how haphazard and inconsistent my prayers are in these areas. I might offer up an "arrow prayer" (a quick, focused plea to God) for the poor if I see a public service announcement on television—but do I regularly include them in daily prayers, along with personal and seemingly more pressing local and community needs? I must admit the answer is no.

Like any of the prayers we offer to our gracious Lord, prayers for government leaders and the related injustices that permeate the chaos that rocks our planet are part of the responsibility entrusted to us. We need to take it seriously and not become apathetic or say to ourselves that we're helpless. "The prayer of a righteous person is powerful and effective," as we read in James 5:16. If the list of world concerns seems too overwhelming to tackle in one fell swoop every time we go before Him in prayer, consider implementing a schedule. Group government leaders together in your prayers for one day, prayers for persecuted Christians and mission teams on another, enslaved and human trafficking victims on another, and so on. By doing this, your prayers are also less rote. You are able to focus fully on the subjects at hand. God, of course, never considers prayers rote even if we sometimes do. When we pray the same prayer, pouring out our whole heart, it doesn't matter how often He's heard it. It's still secured in a golden bowl. What a comfort it is to know this!

⊢━━⊖

Keys to Kingdom Living: Pray authentically and wholeheartedly about world concerns as opposed to inciting divisiveness.

Doorpost: "Instead of the thorn shall come up the cypress; instead of the brier shall come up the myrtle; and it shall make a name for the Lord, an everlasting sign that shall not be cut off." Isaiah 55:13 (ESV)

CONVERT GARDENING: TOOLS FOR SOIL IMPROVEMENT

*E*very good gardener knows his crop is only going to be as good as the soil from which the delicious veggies or beautiful flowers spring. So the good gardener takes care of his precious dirt, making sure he enhances it with robust fertilizer and other enrichments. He keeps it free of weeds that will rob his soil of valuable nutrients and crowd out the desired crop. He bolsters drooping plants with proper supports to give them the best chance of success. Finally, he tries his best to keep predators from devouring or destroying his crop as it matures so it will yield a great bounty in its time.

None of this happens automatically, of course. Good gardeners keep to a strict schedule of sustaining what has been invested. As we "garden" our own hearts and lives, we have a responsibility to make sure the soil from which our crop will produce its yield is healthy enough to sustain growth. We as Christians can fertilize our own soil with a daily application of God's holy Word. We can't help others grow if we aren't growing ourselves. We will need a shovel to dig deep, confessing what is wrong in our own lives and accepting the grace and redemption only Jesus Christ can offer.

A hand pruner will be useful as necessary changes occur in our own lives while praying for real change in the lives of others. God is really the one who does the actual pruning, but we need to yield to what He's doing by complying with the occasionally agonizing process. Finally, a rake will be required to sweep away what is undesirable and worthless. Pick up your rake. We can't afford to let the refuse of our lives to accumulate, crowd out the crop, and take up valuable space. By letting go of past misdeeds and mistakes, we're better able to move forward and be of optimum use to God when all the old debris is swept away.

Once our soil is shipshape, the refuse is cast aside, and we are actively blooming and growing under the Holy Spirit's care, a variety of seeds can be planted in the soil of others. Using our tools, the light of our precious Son, and the living water of the Holy Spirit, we can plant seeds of truth in the parched soil of the brokenhearted. We can plant seeds of encouragement in the lives of those who struggle with addiction. We can plant seeds of hope in those who are chronically or terminally ill. We can plant seeds of joy in the lives of those who struggle as we show them how to overcome any excruciatingly difficult circumstance and hang on to Jesus.

A while back, I was out in my own California yard harvesting oranges. Despite our drought conditions, we were enjoying a bumper crop. As the sun peeked through rain clouds, the Lord spoke to me through what I call an "activity parable": He instructed me to nurture and harvest in my own backyard. He showed me that my community service is part of His plan for my gifts as an encourager and a lover of His people.

***

Keys to Kingdom Living: Enrich your soil so you can get your hands dirty next door.
Doorpost: "Still other seed fell on good soil, where it produced a crop—a hundred, sixty or thirty times what was sown." Matthew 13:8

COVERT GARDENING: THE IMPORTANCE OF LIVING WATER

*hen my older son was little, he had a keen interest in gardening. We would read a storybook about growing a garden full of good and tasty vegetables. His eyes would widen at every reading until finally he told me he didn't want to just read about gardening—he wanted to do it. We got him a pair of overalls and a little gardening hat, and he would putter around outside, removing tomato worms and re-stuffing the scarecrow. He carefully watered his garden until one day the harvest was ready, and voilà! He picked a bumper crop of juicy tomatoes the size of softballs.

Even if the soil is amended and the sun is shining over seeds ready to sprout, a garden won't grow unless it's watered properly. Living water is equally important as we work to plant the seeds of hope into the lives of those who don't know Jesus. Their soil might be ready to receive. You might be ready to deliver the news about the Son. But without the Holy Spirit's presence, growth and change cannot come to pass.

We need to invite the Holy Spirit's presence into our conversations about Jesus. We need a daily watering with God's Word to keep ourselves filled up with what we are trying to give out. Sometimes we neglect to fully internalize the impact the Holy Spirit can make in our lives, especially in our evangelistic efforts. His powerful presence in the holy trinity serves to provide personal support to our own private spiritual life as well as to our public ministries. We read in 2 Corinthians 1:22 and again in 5:5 of how the Holy Spirit bears witness to Jesus, provides liberation from sin and death, and guarantees salvation moving into eternity.

When we are fully aware of this power and invite the Holy Spirit to enhance and bless our endeavors, amazing things take place in our lives and in the lives of others. Before I went to Rwanda, God gave me a vision of my body, my back flat on the dry, cracked, lifeless ground. In the vision, my arms and legs were extended, and water was shooting out of the tips of my fingers. I didn't think much about it at the time, but later I realized that God wanted to use me to bring His living water to His thirsty people in a land where the possession and use of precious water dominates the daunting task of daily living.

People can't live the life God intended without living water, any more than we can physically live without H_2O. It's up to us to serve as the hands and feet of our Redeemer, enlisting the Holy Spirit's help to bring them the good news they so desperately need so they never thirst again.

⊢━━⊕

Keys to Kingdom Living: Lavish your crop of seeds with living water for a harvest that will last forever.
Doorpost: "Whoever drinks of the water that I will give him will never be thirsty again. The water that I will give him will become in him a spring of water welling up to eternal life." John 4:14 (ESV)

COVERT GARDENING: FOR OUR FRIENDS

As we live out our Christian life with purpose, most likely we surround ourselves with friends who fall into one of three categories. We should have friends who mentor us and spur us on to the next level of spiritual growth and ever-maturing faith. We will also be blessed if we cultivate and nurture a life group of people who walk alongside you on your challenging earthly journey. Finally, you should have a targeted group of people—young believers or unbelievers—whom you can mentor and develop into Christ followers.

A friend with any level of significance will probably be brought to mind for prayer at some point. Though good friends will often seek wise counsel from one another, you will probably want to combine secret gardening prayers with the prayers you may engage in with them directly. For instance, a friend who is separated from her husband and hopes to reconcile may ask you to pray for her concern. As you pray with her, you will want to do whatever you can to bolster her spirits and encourage her in your prayer time together. But as you lift her up privately, you may feel led to ask God to strengthen her for comfort in what-ever she might face moving forward, even if the situation will not be resolved to her heart's desire.

Within your circle of friends and family, you may face a variety of challenges with some individuals that may be better confronted through secret gardening. For instance, in my own circle, I had an EGR—Extra Grace Required—couple in it. They struggled in their marriage and, to some degree, in my study group. No course of study or level of interaction seemed to satisfy them. They took turns leading some studies in the group they felt were more in-depth than what had been selected before. Their actions resulted in confusion on the part of other members who felt somehow they didn't measure up.

Looking back on it now, a better course of action would have been to pray for discernment about encouraging them to start their own group or find another group better suited to their needs. Although they did eventually end up leaving our group and going on to another, and yet another after that, I learned from this experience that secret gardening is far more preferable —and effective—than group gossip. We also grow as gardeners, learning to lean into our faith and trust God to do His work as He sees fit.

When it comes to prayer for those we are trying to bring up higher, secret gardening really kicks into high gear. We want to bring our salt and light to those still in the dark, instead of shining a floodlight on their shortcomings or accentuating their misdeeds. That's not to say we need to keep our mouths completely shut if, say, an addict falls off the wagon. In cases like this, our secret gardening needs to involve prayer without ceasing, as Paul talks about in 1 Thessalonians 5:16. We don't need to remind someone every day that we are praying. Like the Nike ad says, "Just do it."

⊢•⊱

Keys to Kingdom Living: Tailor secret gardening according to the desired crop, letting the Master Gardener take the lead.
Doorpost: "Behold, how good and how pleasant it is for brethren to dwell together in unity!" Psalm 133:1 (ESV)

COVERT GARDENING: FOR OUR CHURCH AND OUR PERSONAL MINISTRIES

One of the biggest struggles many churches and ministries face involves getting the quantity and quality of manpower to accomplish growth and change in the group as well as in the lives of its leaders and members. This has been especially true in my local non-denominational Bible study group that serves more than two hundred members. I've seen firsthand the frustrations by those who run it involving how and what to pray for with regard to their own heart's desires.

As we served together, the approach we took was twofold. On our good days, we all prayed fervently and systematically for God's will in the matter of bringing new leaders. We also prayed for the spiritual growth of the class members. Occasionally, deadlines would fast approach when leaders were still needed, and anxiety would rise in the face of goals not met. However, in every situation, the Lord provided, and any perceived needs were met in His way and timing, even if the outcome didn't always look like His praying people thought it should.

Covert gardening isn't always required for prayer coverage of general goals, but it can be a powerful tool in an overall prayer campaign, especially when it comes to changing the one who prays. Nine years ago, a neighboring Bible study that offered a children's program asked for prayer because they only had one teacher, the program director, for eighteen kids. The leader's team engaged in a long corporate prayer campaign to raise up teachers. In an unusual move, they cast a wider net. They even called on neighboring studies in the community (including ours) to join in their prayer. The following year the program's petition resulted in a flood of new teachers, the same ones prayed for by the other group across town.

Gardening for petitions such as church growth, revival, and unity in general are easily prayed out loud in a group. But when it comes to individuals in the ministry, private prayer is almost always the best protocol for improving harmony and effectiveness. For instance, I knew a woman who was highly sensitive and sometimes difficult to work with. Her methods created friction, and some people were in quite a quandary over what to do about the resulting tension. The matter was handled with private prayer, while in general meetings Bible verses were read intended to illuminate to the individual what needed improvement. Fortunately, the individual herself saw what was lacking in her efforts and approach and went about changing it.

That person was, in fact, me! I've been both on the receiving and giving end of secret gardening. However, I must admit this is more of a goal than it is a full-blown achievement. Typically, I would stew and kvetch before praying (and even sometimes after praying). Years and years of living have taught me to try a different tack. As I mature, I'm more inclined to hand matters over to the Lord that I know I've absolutely no control over to let Him do the changing in others as well as in me.

⊷

Keys to Kingdom Living: Secret gardening can effectively bolster corporate prayer efforts.
Doorpost: "Be on guard . . . for all the flock, among which the Holy Spirit made you overseers . . . to shepherd the church of God." Acts 20:28 (NASB)

COVERT GARDENING: THE TRAP
DOORS LEVIED IN THE SPIRITUAL
REALM

The unseen world exists all around us. There are efforts from on high to encourage and sustain us in the unseen world. These are helpful and intended for good by God. Others are evil and dispatched by Satan to wreak havoc and destruction. Again, because they are unseen, it's much easier to fall through the trap door you never saw coming.

You might be wondering why it is that believers aren't privy to viewing the unseen world. Why aren't we permitted to see all the evil that goes on, as well as the beautiful protection on the part of angels? I believe that our inability to see the horrors of the Enemy's activities is a blessing from God. Prophets like Ezekiel and Daniel were often distressed over what they saw with regard to visions and abominations. Regardless of the reason, we need to be mindful that the unseen world is very real, as are God's efforts to protect and preserve us though His angels.

We learn about godly intervention in the story of Balaam as recorded in Numbers 22. God told Balaam not to go to Egypt, but Balaam was enticed by a monetary reward that awaited him there. He disobeyed God and began his journey. God dispatched an angel with a sword and placed it at the end of the road where Balaam was traveling. Along the way, the Lord stopped his donkey. God literally spoke through the donkey's mouth. The merciful act was meant to save Balaam from the destruction from the very angel God had commissioned. When the Lord opened Balaam's eyes, Balaam understood the gravity of his actions, so he hit the ground and bowed before God. In His infinite grace and mercy, God opened Balaam's eyes.

As we know from Scripture, the Enemy seeks destruction, not growth. He is no gardener. He wants to lay our spiritual landscapes bare. In Daniel 10:13 we learn about the angel Michael who was preoccupied for twenty-one days in the kingdom of Persia battling invisible forces of evil. We are told in Ephesians 6:12 that we wrestle against "the cosmic powers of this present darkness, against the spiritual forces of evil in the heavenly places" (ESV).

I believe we're continually protected by angels from a variety of dangers that we are completely unaware of. Your annoying five-minute delay leaving the house may have prevented your car from being a part of an accident. The seemingly devastating breakup with your fiancé may have protected you from a life of misery. Because we indeed cannot see everything, we need to trust God in all circumstances because only He is privy to the seen and unseen worlds and He is trustworthy to help us journey along, avoiding a myriad of traps and pitfalls. By focusing on good and perfect gifts that come from above, we can help keep the weeds of the Enemy from taking over our soil. And if we hold fast to His Word and leading, we can sidestep trap doors and succeed in avoiding the Abyss as our final destination.

Keys to Kingdom Living: Thank God for all the ways his angels preserve you.

Doorpost: "The angel of the Lord encamps around those who fear him, and he delivers them." Psalm 34:7

ACKNOWLEDGMENTS

How amazing is our God, who saw fit to take ten months of writing and multiply it "loaves and fishes" style into three separate books. Much to my surprise, writing the second book turned out to be difficult in different areas than the first one did. I actually found myself unexpectedly falling through a trap door of my own I never saw coming. A special thank you to those who reminded me of the redemptive work of our Kinsman Redeemer and reached into my abyss to help me out—in particular, Jan Moorad, Judy Jennemann, and Doreen Fincher.

A special thanks to Marilyn Hewlett, my Bible study friend and fellow dim sum enthusiast who offered to check the many Scriptural references found in the text.

To my husband of thirty-six years, Ben Yorks, who faithfully and generously supports me both financially and spiritually to continue to help me spread my messages of encouragement to those who need to hear them.

To the amazing Maryam Siahatgar, whose amazing graphic design artistry is responsible for both published books in The Door trilogy.

And last, but certainly not least, to the incomparable Jody Skinner! Her sharp editing skills, technical expertise, and deep reverence for God's holy word make her an ideal *confrere* in the self-publishing arena. More sister than colleague, she's been there to encourage and inspire when I was dangling from my last participle over the precipice of self doubt. No amount of thanks can begin to express my deep gratitude for her many gifts.

And to all who prayed and cheered me on, and who continue to support, encourage, and share my materials with those who need them—a heartfelt thank you.

You can find Cindy at www.cindyyorks.com or on her social media accounts. Please drop by and say hello!

facebook.com/cindylafavre.yorks

instagram.com/cindy_lafavre_yorks

NOTES

3. THE TRAP DOOR: ABUNDANCE & SELF-RELIANCE

1. Sinatra, Frank. My Way. Reprise, 1969, LP.
2. "Shirley MacLaine Quote." n.d. AZ Quotes. Accessed October 1, 2019. https://www.azquotes.com/quote/182507.
3. "Kip Pardue Quotes." n.d. QuotesGram. Accessed October 1, 2019. https://quotesgram.com/kip-pardue-quotes/.

6. THE TRAP DOOR: HELPLESSNESS AND DEFEATISM

1. Van Sutphin, Priscilla. 2009. "Overcoming Defeatism." Upstream Ministries. May 5, 2009. http://www.upstreamca.org/oc_defeatism.html.

7. TWISTING: TO THE RIGHT TO HELP ENCOURAGE THE SHEEP

1. Ward, William Arthur. n.d. "William Arthur Ward - Flatter Me, and I May..." Inspirational Words of Wisdom. Accessed October 2, 2019. https://www.wow4u.com/william-arthur-ward2/.

1. ABANDON: IGNORING OUR AGENDA TO CLING TO HIS

1. Vasel, Kathryn. 2017. "It Costs $233,610 to Raise a Child." CNNMoney. Cable News Network. January 9, 2017. https://money.cnn.com/2017/01/09/pf/cost-of-raising-a-child-2015/index.html.
2. O'Donnell, Shannon. 2019. "A Little RTW Budget... How Much Does It Cost to Travel the World for a Year? (2019)." A Little Adrift. May 15, 2019. https://alittleadrift.com/rtw-budget-travel-around-the-world/.
3. Teresa, Mother. n.d. "Mother Teresa Quote." AZ Quotes. Accessed October 2, 2019. https://www.azquotes.com/quote/418071.

3. ABANDON: GIVING UP A NEST OF EAGLES TO WELCOME BABY BIRDS

1. Logothetis, Leon. 2017. "Keeping Good Company: Why You Should Surround Yourself With Good People." HuffPost. HuffPost. December 7, 2017. https://www.huffpost.com/entry/kkeeping-good-company-why-you-should-surround-yourself-with-good-people_b_6816468.

4. INJUSTICE: HOW TO BATTLE AGAINST IT

1. Herbert, Bob. "In America; A Sea Change On Crime." The New York Times, December 12, 1993, sec. 4. https://www.nytimes.com/1993/12/12/opinion/in-america-a-sea-change-on-crime.html.
2. Jones, Mary Harris. n.d. "Mother Jones Quotes." QuotesGram. Accessed October 2, 2019. https://quotesgram.com/mother-jones-quotes/.
3. Tutu, Desmond. n.d. "Desmond Tutu." Motto'd. Accessed October 2, 2019. https://mottod.com/authors/desmond-tutu.

5. INJUSTICE: MAKING AMENDS WITHIN MINISTRIES AND CHRISTIAN FRIENDSHIPS

1. Metzger, Bruce M. 2012. *Textual Commentary on the Greek New Testament.* Stuttgart Deutschebibelgesellschaft.

2. FAILURE: THE TRAP OF NON-FORGIVENESS

1. King, Martin Luther. 1957. Christmas sermon, December 25. https://findingforgiveness.blogspot.com/2009/01/martin-luther-king-on-forgiveness.html.

6. FAILURE: AS A PRECURSOR FOR REBIRTH AND RENEWAL

1. Garson. 2019. "Our Greatest Glory Is Not in Never Falling, But in Rising Every Time We Fall." Quote Investigator. January 3, 2019. https://quoteinvestigator.com/2014/05/27/rising/.

7. COMBATTING LONELINESS: ELEANOR RIGBY AND BEYOND

1. The Beatles. 1966. *Revolver.*

4. DODGING SELF-ESTEEM BARBS: THE FAILURE TRAP

1. Canfield, Jack (@JackCanfield). "Everything you want is on the other side of fear. http://ow.ly/i/1QIZq" 9 Apr. 2013, 6:21 a.m. Tweet.

2. WHOPPERS FROM PULPIT AND PEW: PRAY HARD ENOUGH, GOD WILL ANSWER YOUR WAY

1. Joplin, Janis. Mercedes Benz. Sunset Sound Recorders, 1970.

ISBN (paperback): 978-0-9980481-1-6

⊢━━⮾